International Curriculum
for Chinese Language Education

国际汉语教学通用课程大纲

国家汉语国际推广领导小组办公室
The Office of Chinese Language Council International

外语教学与研究出版社
FOREIGN LANGUAGE TEACHING AND RESEARCH PRESS
北京　BEIJING

图书在版编目(CIP)数据

国际汉语教学通用课程大纲 ＝ International Curriculum for Chinese Language Education：英汉
对照／国家汉语国际推广领导小组办公室编．— 北京：外语教学与研究出版社，2008.3
ISBN 978－7－5600－7401－6

Ⅰ．国…　Ⅱ．国…　Ⅲ．对外汉语教学—教学大纲　Ⅳ．H195.2

中国版本图书馆 CIP 数据核字（2008）第 037862 号

出　版　人：于春迟
责任编辑：潘瑞芳
封面设计：张　峰
版式设计：平　原
出版发行：外语教学与研究出版社
社　　　址：北京市西三环北路 19 号（100089）
网　　　址：http://www.fltrp.com
印　　　刷：中国农业出版社印刷厂
开　　　本：787×1092　1/16
印　　　张：17　插页 1 张
版　　　次：2008 年 3 月第 1 版　2010 年 3 月第 5 次印刷
书　　　号：ISBN 978－7－5600－7401－6
定　　　价：49.00 元
＊　　＊　　＊
如有印刷、装订质量问题，请与出版社联系
联系电话：(010)61207896　　电子邮箱：zhijian@fltrp.com
制售盗版必究 举报查实奖励
版权保护办公室举报电话：(010)88817519
物料号：174010001

Chen Xiaoming   (Beijing Foreign Studies University)

Robert S. Chen   (Canadian TCSL Association, Canada)

Chen Xin   (Fangcaodi Primary School, Beijing)

Michael Everson   (University of Iowa, USA)

Sue Jollow   (Chinese Language Teachers' Association,
                     Victoria, Australia)

Maeng, Joo-oeck   (Hankuk University of Foreign Studies, Korea)

Yue Wei   (Beijing Foreign Studies University)

Lin Xiuqin   (Capital Normal University)

Yulan Lin   (Chinese Language Association of Secondary-
                     Elementary Schools, USA)

Wu Juan   (Beijing Foreign Studies University)

Zheng Meiying   (No.55 High School of Beijing)

Tao-chung Yao   (University of Hawaii, USA)

Si Chung Mou   (The University of Hong Kong)

Peter Kupfer   (University Mainz, Germany)

David Holm   (University of Melbourne, Australia)

He Jun   (Beijing Foreign Studies University)

Zhao Jing   (Beijing Language and Culture University)

Zhao Jinming   (Beijing Language and Culture University)

Zhao Yong   (Michigan State University, USA)

Zhao Xuemei   (Beijing Language and Culture University)

Xu Hong   (Edmonton Public School Board, Canada)

Sandy Forster   (Edmonton Public School Board, Canada)

Qian Suping   (Penleigh & Essendon Grammar School, Australia)

Neil Kubler   (Williams College, USA)

Cui Yonghua   (Beijing Language and Culture University)

Cui Songren   (Bowdoin College, USA)

Liang Dongmei	(Beijing Foreign Studies University)
Liang Yanmin	(Beijing Language and Culture University)
Gong Yafu	(People's Education Press)
Miao-Fen Tseng	(University of Virginia, USA)
Xie Mianmian	(Edmonton Public School Board, Canada)
Han Xi	(International Languages Aotearoa, New Zealand)
Tan Chunjian	(Beijing Language and Culture University)
Wei Hongxia	(State of Victoria Department of Education and Early Childhood Development, Australia)
Wei Chongxin	(Beijing Foreign Studies University)

Introduction

1. Objectives

In compliance with the rapid development of Chinese language education around the world, *International Curriculum for Chinese Language Education* (hereafter called ICCLE) has been developed under the auspices of Hanban/Confucius Institute Headquarters to meet the needs of many countries for standardizing Chinese language education.

As an organiser and a descriptor of objectives and content of Chinese language curriculum, ICCLE strives to provide a reference curriculum for Chinese language educational agencies and instructors in their planning, to establish a framework for assessing language competence of Chinese language learners, and to offer a basis for Chinese language resource development in further promotion of Chinese language education.

2. Principles for ICCLE

2.1　Scientificality

ICCLE uses as its theoretical guideline the language competence in communication, absorbing rich experiences of Chinese language education both at home and abroad. It has benefited widely from experiences and achievements in foreign and second language education globally, and has been developed on large-scale and thorough scientific research in both past experiences and current practices, thus assuring its scientificality, timeliness, and logicality based on extensive theories and positive practices.

2.2　Practicality

ICCLE serves as a practical guidance in international Chinese language education, elaborating in detail on different levels of linguistic skills, knowledge, strategies, and cultural awareness required by curriculum and the learner. At the same time, ICCLE incorporates as valuable references a variety of appendices, including (1) *Recommended Themes and Topics for Chinese Language Teaching,* (2) *CLT Subjects, Objectives and Sample Arrangements,* (3) *Subjects and Learning Objectives on Chinese Culture,* (4) *Sample Activities for Chinese Language Teaching,* (5) *Grammatical Items,* (6) *Phonetic System of Chinese Language,* (7) *List of 800 Common Characters,* and (8) *List of 1,500 Frequent Words*[1]. ICCLE and its appendices have supplied users with a plethora of resources to be adapted, to be selected, or to be modified in order to suit the diversified teaching and learning situations. It can also be

---

1　The last three appendices can be seen in the Chinese edition on P. 97–123.

customised for syllabus design or textbook compilation.

2.3 Intentionality

International Chinese language education has started to move from an ivory tower towards popularity, commonality, and practicality. In this edition of the ICCLE we have strived to cater for a variety of Chinese language learners, especially students at primary and high schools, as well as people from all walks of life. Difficulties of Chinese language learning have been considerably reduced and objectives and skills have been adjusted to suit more novice learners. Communicative abilities have been emphasised to meet the actual needs in international Chinese language education.

2.4 Suitability

With reference to a few of the world-renowned standards, such as *Chinese Language Proficiency Scales for Speakers of Other Languages* and *Common European Framework of Reference for Languages: Learning, Teaching, Assessment*, for their cross-cultural perspectives, ICCLE has as well absorbed current achievements and experiences in international Chinese language education. Chinese linguistic knowledge and cultural knowledge have been reorganised in ICCLE and many examples have been suggested for educators in international Chinese language education to apply in their teaching, teacher education, and textbook compilation projects.

3. Contents

3.1 General Objectives

International Chinese language education aims to help learners with their Chinese language knowledge and skills, including consolidation of their intentions to learn Chinese language, self-direction and cooperation, effective learning strategies, and the ultimate goal of comprehensive mastery of linguistic competencies.

Linguistic competencies are composed of linguistic knowledge, linguistic skills, strategies, and cultural awareness, with the former two functioning as the basis. Strategies act as conditions upon which learners increase their efficiency, learn independently, and develop their personal abilities. Cultural awareness guarantees the development of a global learner in his or her appropriate use of a language in a pluricultural society.

The interrelatedness of the four components of linguistic competencies is exemplified in the following figure.

Structure of ICCLE

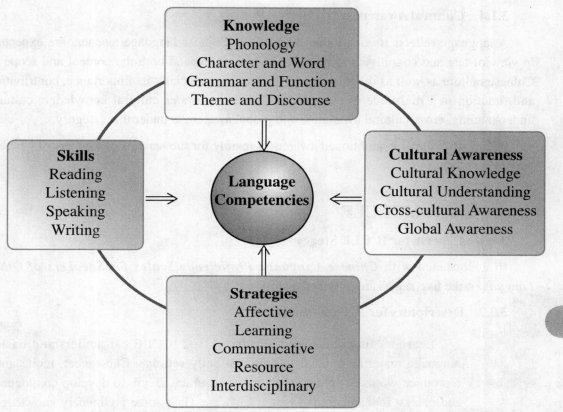

Knowledge
Phonology
Character and Word
Grammar and Function
Theme and Discourse

Skills
Reading
Listening
Speaking
Writing

Language Competencies

Cultural Awareness
Cultural Knowledge
Cultural Understanding
Cross-cultural Awareness
Global Awareness

Strategies
Affective
Learning
Communicative
Resource
Interdisciplinary

3.1.1 Linguistic Knowledge

As an integral component of linguistic competencies, linguistic knowledge provides an indispensable foundation for the four skills of reading, listening, speaking and writing. ICCLE has categorised linguistic knowledge into six facets, phonology, character and word, grammar, function, theme, and discourse.

3.1.2 Linguistic Skills

Linguistics skills form an important component of linguistic performance. ICCLE has outlined both general and specific outcomes regarding the "Big Four" of reading, listening, speaking, writing, and relevant subskills.

3.1.3 Strategies

Strategies are further divided into affective, learning (both cognitive and metacognitive strategies), communicative, resource, and interdisciplinary strategies.

ICCLE lists the aforementioned strategies mainly for the benefits of teachers of Chinese language and culture.

3.1.4　Cultural Awareness

A language reflects its rich cultural heritages. Chinese language teachers are expected, in view of age and cognitive ability of the learner, to expand both the content and scope of Chinese culture as well as the horizons of the learner, especially its importance, contribution and function in a multitude of cultures. ICCLE incorporates cultural knowledge, cultural understanding, cross-cultural awareness and global awareness under this category.

ICCLE lists the aforementioned awareness mainly for the benefits of teachers of Chinese language and culture.

3.2　Stages of ICCLE

3.2.1　Criteria for ICCLE Stages

In accordance with *Chinese Language Proficiency Scales for Speakers of Other Languages*, the five stages are provided as follows.

3.2.2　Descriptors for ICCLE Stages

Stage 1	Learners functioning within Stage 1 of ICCLE can understand basic language materials related to common daily settings. Can repeat, recite and reproduce words or sentences with fair accuracy. Begin to develop confidence and interest in learning the Chinese language. Have some preliminary knowledge of learning strategies, communicative strategies, resource strategies and interdisciplinary strategies used in guided situations. Gain introductory Chinese cultural knowledge and acquire preliminary cross-cultural awareness and international perspectives.
Stage 2	Learners functioning within Stage 2 of ICCLE can understand and master basic language materials related to common daily settings. Can produce simple sentence structures, provide simple descriptions, and exchange some basic information. Begin to develop confidence and interest in learning the Chinese language. Have some preliminary knowledge of learning strategies, communicative strategies, resource strategies and interdisciplinary strategies. Gain introductory Chinese cultural knowledge, and acquire preliminary cross-cultural awareness and international perspectives.

Stage 3	Learners functioning within Stage 3 of ICCLE can understand and learn language related to daily settings. Can use more complex grammatical structures and sentence patterns to communicate on familiar topics through interaction and description. Can compose brief passages. Demonstrate confidence and interest in learning the Chinese language. Have some preliminary knowledge of learning strategies, communicative strategies, resource strategies and interdisciplinary strategies used in guided situations. Gain introductory Chinese cultural knowledge and acquire preliminary cross-cultural awareness and international perspectives.
Stage 4	Learners functioning within Stage 4 of ICCLE can understand language materials within sectors of social life. Can produce more correct sentences on familiar topics in description, explanation or comparison. Can compose simple passages or connect basic passages. Have demonstrated confidence and interest in learning the Chinese language. Have mastered some knowledge of learning strategies, communicative strategies, resource strategies and interdisciplinary strategies. Have gained introductory Chinese cultural knowledge and acquired preliminary cross-cultural awareness and international perspectives.
Stage 5	Learners functioning within Stage 5 of ICCLE can understand a wide range of topics, produce correct sentences, write in paragraphs, create cohesive discourse, express themselves fluently and spontaneously without much obvious searching for expressions. Have demonstrated confidence and a strong interest in learning the Chinese language. Have mastered knowledge with learning strategies, communicative strategies, resource strategies and interdisciplinary strategies. Have gained extensive Chinese cultural knowledge and acquired preliminary cross-cultural awareness and international perspectives.

4. For What Users Is ICCLE Intended?

ICCLE is designed to be used by educators in international Chinese language education, as well as learners of the Chinese language, from preschoolers to adults, from school to non-school learners, irrespective of their language background. School learners can refer to those educated at public schools (primary, junior, and senior high schools), at separate schools, at private schools, or at international schools. Non-school learners refer to those taking lessons for their personal interests at evening schools, at weekend schools, or at extension schools. Teachers of Chinese to speakers of other languages and volunteer teachers will find ICCLE a valuable reference in their careers, and ICCLE also serves as a source and guide for Chinese textbook compilers.

5. The Making of ICCLE

Since the beginning of 2007, Hanban/Confucius Institute Headquarters has commissioned 300 language educational experts and teachers to participate in the research on and the design of ICCLE. For data collection, preliminary research, feedback from pilot studies, drafting and revision of ICCLE contributed by Chinese language teacher associations, Confucius Institutes, and local Chinese language teaching institutes in Canada, the United States, the United Kingdom, France, Australia, Japan, South Korea, Germany, Russia, Columbia, and Singapore, we express our deepest indebtedness.

The editorial board is grateful to translators whose contributions made this document possible. Special thanks go to Mr. Feng Rui (Canada) for Introduction and Chapters One to Five; Ms. Zhang Lixin for Appendices 1 and 2; Ms. Peng Lin for Appendix 3; Mr. Fan Haixiang for Appendix 4; and Ms. Wu Xiaobo for Appendix 5.

Due to time constraints and lack of thorough research, ICCLE is bound to have inadequacies. The Office is hoping to approach perfection in such a developing project. Readers are invited to supply us with suggestions for the improvement of the next edition.

Hanban/Confucius Institute Headquarters

Beijing, China

March 2008

Table of Contents

International Curriculum
for Chinese Language Education

Chapter One   Stage 1 Objectives and Content

1.1   Objectives

Learners functioning within Stage 1 of ICCLE can understand basic language materials related to common daily settings. Can repeat, recite and reproduce words or sentences with fair accuracy. Begin to develop confidence and interest in learning the Chinese language. Have some preliminary knowledge of learning strategies, communicative strategies, resource strategies and interdisciplinary strategies used in guided situations. Gain introductory Chinese cultural knowledge and acquire preliminary cross-cultural awareness and international perspectives.

1.2   Linguistic Knowledge

Knowledge	Description of Objectives
Phonology	1. listen to, identify and produce the basic sounds of *Pinyin* (Chinese Phonetic Alphabet, CPA); 2. begin to identify Chinese character pronunciations; 3. know that Chinese is a tonal language and Putonghua (common speech) has four tones and a neutral tone.
Character and Word	With teacher guidance: 1. master 150 common Chinese characters (ideograms) toward proficiency in the four skills areas of reading, listening, speaking and writing; 2. recognise basic components of characters and radicals; 3. recognise strokes and stroke order of characters; 4. understand the relationships between characters and words; 5. master 300 words related to daily life and school life.
Grammar	Know and master: 1. basic word order; 2. common sentence patterns, general questions and negative sentences with 不; 3. common nouns, numerals and measure words; 4. personal pronouns and demonstratives; 5. basic expressions to describe a person or an object; 6. common verbs, adjectives and adverbs of dagree.

Knowledge	Description of Objectives
Function	1. know major communicative functions such as greetings, thanks, apologies and farewells; 2. use body language or material objects to enhance everyday communication situations.
Theme	1. master basic and simple ways of social interaction; 2. know simple topics related to family and personal life, or hobbies; 3. know simple topics related to everyday life, such as numbers, time, dates and currency.
Discourse	With teacher guidance: 1. know sentences in their proper use and longer passages; understand the stream of thought (priorities); 2. learn to understand the stem of a sentence; understand simple sentences via modifiers and limiters; 3. perceive differences and contrasts in thinking between Chinese language and learners' mother tongue; 4. perceive figures of speech in Chinese; 5. understand emotions expressed in both written and spoken Chinese.

1.3 Linguistic Skills

Skills	Description of Objectives
General	Can understand basic, simple and limited language materials closely related to personal and daily activities, with occasional help of body language, material objects and proper context. Can understand titles and some daily greetings. Can introduce themselves or communicate with others using a very limited vocabulary.

	Skills	Description of Objectives
Specific	**Listening**	Can understand basic, familiar and well-pronounced words, simple sentences and classroom expressions related to personal and daily activities. Can guess or deduce the meaning or intention of the speaker with the help of body language or context and respond accordingly, including: 1. very limited and brief expressions related to personal and daily life; 2. basic numerals; 3. simple greetings and methods of addressing people; 4. basic classroom expressions or instructions; 5. simple requests.
	Speaking	Can repeat, retell and recite words and sentences learned. Can respond to simple greetings. Can address new acquaintances and introduce themselves. Can exchange some basic personal information. Can indicate basic needs and wants, with the help of body language or material objects when needed, including: 1. repeat, retell and recite words and sentences learned in class with proper tones; 2. exchange basic personal information; 3. initiate and respond to greetings; 4. give and respond to simple instructions and commands; 5. make simple requests and seek assistance.
	Reading	Can recognise *Pinyin* and some simple characters, words and numbers learned in class in the exchange of personal information, including: 1. recognise *Pinyin* and use *Pinyin* to locate characters with the help of dictionaries; 2. extract specific information in simple everyday contexts related to personal and daily life from brief discourse; 3. understand common greetings and expressions of gratitude in social interactions; 4. understand common characters, words and numbers related to daily activities; 5. understand commonly seen signs and instructions with the help of drawings and photos.

5

Skills		Description of Objectives
Specific	**Writing**	Can rewrite fairly correctly basic characters learned in class. Can compose simple phrases and sentences in *Pinyin*, including: 1. copy with correct stroke order; 2. enter name and nationality on a form; 3. write simple everyday expressions, dates, time or previously learned numbers; 4. use some simple text forms in their own productions, e.g., cards, in social interactions correctly.

1.4   Strategies

Strategies	Description of Objectives
Affective	1. cultivate a desire for and an interest in Chinese language; 2. cultivate confidence in learning Chinese and demonstrate willingness to use Chinese; 3. reduce anxiety when an error is made.
Learning	1. explore simple classification systems and criteria for categories; 2. try to mimic what the teacher says; 3. integrate old knowledge strategically with new knowledge; 4. make sentences with isolated words; 5. respond to suggestions for revising their own work; 6. learn to make their own study plans; 7. learn to seek help from others when in difficulties.
Communicative	1. use simple affective strategies to enhance language learning, observe and imitate practices that are common among Chinese people; 2. with teacher guidance, interact with other classmates and teachers to understand common etiquettes in Chinese culture; 3. with teacher guidance, use non-linguistic conventions (gesture or mime) to enhance communication.
Resource	1. with teacher guidance, learn to use textbooks, pictures, pictionaries and multimedia resources to seek information; 2. with teacher guidance, learn to obtain learning resources via teachers and classmates.

Strategies	Description of Objectives
Interdisciplinary	1. with teacher guidance, expand one's personal knowledge base and learn to relate information obtained in Chinese language and culture to their learning of other subjects; 2. with teacher guidance, learn to relate the information studied in other subjects to their learning of Chinese language and culture; learn the importance of overall language ability; 3. this stage covers music, fine arts, history and folklores.

1.5   Cultural Awareness

Awareness	Description of Objectives
Cultural Knowledge	1. know the benefits of using different languages locally; 2. understand development and achievement in education and culture locally and in China; 3. learn to know cuisine and costumes of Chinese culture; 4. know the essence of simple Chinese stories, allusion making and connotation; 5. know both linguistic and non-linguistic means of communication in Chinese culture; 6. know simple social etiquettes and customs in Chinese culture; 7. know interpersonal relations in Chinese culture.
Cultural Understanding	1. develop interest in Chinese culture; 2. experience Chinese cultural elements and understand the relationships between culture and language learning; 3. experience the Chinese cultural value-systems; 4. experience cultural multiplicity and permeability between cultures.
Cross-cultural Awareness	1. examine commonalities and differences between Chinese culture and their own culture; 2. learn the importance of cross-cultural awareness via Chinese culture.
Global Awareness	1. experience cultural phenomena in China and locally; 2. learn to view the world from different perspectives via learning about Chinese language and culture; 3. experience global citizenship.

Chapter Two Stage 2 Objectives and Content

2.1 Objectives

Learners functioning within Stage 2 of ICCLE can understand and master basic language materials related to common daily settings. Can produce simple sentence structures, provide simple descriptions, and exchange some basic information. Begin to develop confidence and interest in learning the Chinese language. Have some preliminary knowledge of learning strategies, communicative strategies, resource strategies and interdisciplinary strategies. Gain introductory Chinese cultural knowledge, and acquire preliminary cross-cultural awareness and international perspectives.

2.2 Linguistic Knowledge

Knowledge	Description of Objectives
Phonology	1. know the importance of pronunciation in learning Chinese language; 2. master some tone changes; 3. use appropriate pronunciation and intonation in everyday conversation.
Character and Word	1. master 300 common Chinese characters (ideograms) toward proficiency in the four skills areas; 2. identify sounds, forms and meanings of Chinese characters; 3. understand the relationships between characters and words; 4. master 600 words related to daily life and school life.
Grammar	Know and master: 1. RMB, sum of money and interrogative pronouns; 2. expressions of time, place and location; 3. special questions; 4. structures and functions of attributes and adverbials; 5. existential sentences; 6. expressions of wishes.

Knowledge	Description of Objectives
Function	1. know major communicative functions such as greetings, thanks, apologies and farewells; 2. know and use communicative functions such as inquiries, introductions and descriptions; 3. accomplish simple daily interactions.
Theme	1. know topics of personal interest and family life; 2. know topics of daily and leisure activities; 3. know simple topics of campus and professional life.
Discourse	With teacher guidance: 1. know sentences in their proper context and produce longer passages; 2. know the parts of a sentence and learn to master the stem of a sentence and understand connotations via modifiers and limiters; 3. perceive differences and contrasts in thinking between Chinese language and learners' mother tongue; 4. perceive figures of speech in Chinese (hyperbole, parallelism); 5. understand emotions expressed in both written and spoken Chinese.

9

2.3   Linguistic Skills

Skills	Description of Objectives
General	Can understand simple language materials closely related to personal and daily activities. Can communicate with others on such topics and introduce themselves or others. Can understand simple words and phrases used to express emotions and feelings (thanks or apologies) and attitudes (positive or negative); know how to exchange greetings and farewells in different contexts.

Skills		Description of Objectives
Specific	Listening	Can understand basic materials closely related to personal and daily activities and seek relevant information. Can understand classroom interactions and respond to instructions accordingly, including: 1. brief expressions related to personal and daily life; 2. casual exchange of phrases and greetings; 3. brief questions, replies, demands or requests related to personal and daily life; 4. numbers, time or place mentioned in conversation; 5. classroom directions.
	Speaking	Can reproduce sentences in appropriate tone and give simple answers to questions. Can communicate with others on topics closely related to personal and daily activities. Can express personal needs and wants, including: 1. use simple vocabulary to exchange basic information about themselves and others; 2. communicate with others, using simple words and phrases, on topics closely related to personal and daily activities; ask simple questions or respond with clear answers; 3. communicate with others in familiar situations, using previously learned words and phrases; give simple instructions or make simple requests; express needs and seek assistance; 4. appropriately express attitudes and emotions on different occasions.
	Reading	Can recognise basic characters, words, sentences and short textual materials, understand program requirements and gather relevant information from short textual materials, including: 1. recognise the general idea of simple informational materials related to personal and daily activities; 2. recognise and understand greetings, thanks, or invitations in routine social interactions; 3. guess the meaning of signs, symbols or descriptive materials encountered in daily activities written in familiar characters and words; 4. understand simple notes, notices, graphs, tables and lists; 5. locate specific information in short and easy materials with fixed structures.

Skills		Description of Objectives
Specific	Writing	Can write from memory basic characters, with correct strokes and stroke order. Can form new sentences, including: 1. use simple vocabulary to give information relevant to their own lives; 2. use simple vocabulary or sentences to express thanks, apologies, congratulations and farewells; 3. write down basic information closely related to family or personal life; 4. write down short answers to questions closely related to personal life.

2.4   Strategies

Strategies	Description of Objectives
Affective	1. keep interested in Chinese language; take part in activities which help them to improve their language competence; 2. increase confidence in learning Chinese; communicate and express themselves in Chinese; 3. learn to reduce anxiety by different techniques.
Learning	1. experience Chinese language learning and concentrate on language input; 2. learn Chinese through various methods of Chinese language acquisition; 3. obtain and memorise information with the help of imagination; maximize effectiveness by imaging or divergent thinking; 4. make sentences with isolated words; take notes on visual information and report in verbal information; 5. adapt to learning environment and seek advice on strategies for solving their problems; 6. with teacher guidance, discover their own learning methods and learn to make their own study plans; 7. learn to preview and review; 8. learn to create/establish or select a good learning environment.

Strategies	Description of Objectives
Communicative	1. use simple affective strategies to improve learning efficiency and seek assistance; 2. interact in Chinese language with classmates, teachers or friends both in and outside of classroom; 3. with teacher guidance, use non-linguistic conventions (gesture or mime) to enhance communication; experience common etiquettes and customs in Chinese culture.
Resource	1. with teacher guidance, learn to use textbooks, pictionaries, dictionaries, libraries and online databases to seek needed information and resources; 2. learn to obtain learning resources via teachers, classmates, schools, or communities.
Interdisciplinary	1. expand their personal knowledge base; 2. learn that the study of Chinese language and culture has given a fresh impetus to their learning of other subjects; 3. learn to relate the information obtained in other subjects to their learning of Chinese language and culture; 4. learn the importance of overall ability; 5. this stage covers history, folklore, fine arts, etc.

2.5 Cultural Awareness

Awareness	Description of Objectives
Cultural Knowledge	1. know that individuals have the right to learn different languages; 2. understand development and achievements in education and culture locally and in China; 3. experience Chinese culture, arts, festivals and celebrations; 4. know the essence of simple Chinese stories, allusion making and connotation; 5. know both linguistic and non-linguistic means of communication in Chinese culture; 6. know simple social etiquettes and customs in Chinese culture; 7. know interpersonal relations in Chinese culture; 8. learn Chinese people's contributions to the society in the country where they live.

Awareness	Description of Objectives
Cultural Understanding	1. understand that culture is not only acquired, it is also learned via language; 2. know the relationships between culture and language learning, the latter being one important component of the former; 3. understand basic value-systems in Chinese culture; 4. experience cultural multiplicity, dynamics and permeability between cultures.
Cross-cultural Awareness	1. examine commonalities and differences between Chinese culture and their own culture; 2. learn the importance of cross-cultural awareness via learning about Chinese culture; 3. learn to view their own culture more objectively by engaging in comparisons between some elements of Chinese culture with their own.
Global Awareness	1. attach importance to increased global perspectives via learning Chinese language; 2. begin to recognize the importance of viewing the world from different perspectives via learning Chinese culture; 3. begin to develop a sense of global citizenship.

Chapter Three   Stage 3 Objectives and Content

3.1   Objectives

Learners functioning within Stage 3 of ICCLE can understand and learn language related to daily settings. Can use more complex grammatical structures and sentence patterns to communicate on familiar topics through interaction and description. Can compose brief passages. Demonstrate confidence and interest in learning the Chinese language. Have some preliminary knowledge of learning strategies, communicative strategies, resource strategies and interdisciplinary strategies used in guided situations. Gain introductory Chinese cultural knowledge and acquire preliminary cross-cultural awareness and international perspectives.

3.2   Linguistic Knowledge

Knowledge	Description of Objectives
Phonology	1. listen to, identify and produce the basic sounds of *Pinyin* (Chinese Phonetic Alphabet, CPA); 2. use *Pinyin* to learn to pronounce unfamiliar words and sentences; 3. understand in connected speech intonation patterns, tone changes, etc., within daily settings; 4. use appropriate pronunciation and intonation in everyday conversation.
Character and Word	1. master 450 common Chinese characters (ideograms) toward proficiency in the four skills areas; 2. recognise basic components of characters and radicals; 3. identify sounds, forms and meanings of Chinese characters; 4. use appropriate semantic cueing system to understand meanings of words; 5. use appropriate words, phrases and expressions in interactions; 6. master 900 words related to daily life, school life and the workplace.
Grammar	Know and master: 1. common modal verbs and prepositions; 2. comparative structures; 3. progressive aspect; 4. particle 了; 5. negative sentences with 没有.

Knowledge	Description of Objectives
Function	1. apply familiar communicative functions in different situations; 2. understand and apply macrofunctions such as exposition, narration and description; 3. communicate with a degree of fluency and spontaneity in daily life, school life and the workplace.
Theme	1. know further topics of personal interest and daily life; 2. know simple topics related to personal environment, school life and the workplace; 3. know simple topics related to social and cultural activities in Chinese culture.
Discourse	1. perceive differences and similarities in train of thought between Chinese language and learners' mother tongue; 2. learn to master the main sentence stem and understand connotations via modifiers and limiters; 3. try to apply simple rhetoric devices and recognise more complex ones; 4. learn how emotions are expressed in both spoken and written Chinese, based on features and functions of simple rhetoric devices.

3.3   Linguistic Skills

Skills	Description of Objectives
General	Can understand basic language materials closely related to personal and school activities common in social interactions. Can communicate with others on such familiar topics, and compose simple passages. Can develop increased effectiveness in communicating with others with the help of stresses, pauses, intonation or body language.

15

Skills		Description of Objectives
Specific	**Listening**	Can understand simple dialogues and statements closely related to personal and daily activities; understand common exchanges and requests to meet basic needs in personal and school life, including: 1. understand gists of dialogues and short speech related to daily and school life; understand the general idea; 2. identify key words or phrases in a speech; 3. understand brief dialogues or conversations related to personal life and experience; 4. understand commonsensical and simple questions; 5. identify basic information in small talk, introductions or phone conversations; 6. understand gists of simple stories.
	Speaking	Can take part in simple conversations and express personal opinions or needs; reproduce more complex sentences and provide simple descriptions of familiar things, events or routine happenings, including: 1. learn to emphasise by stressing particular sounds or by using pauses, intonation or body language; 2. take part in simple or routine conversations on personal needs and wants; 3. interact with others or make statements on familiar topics related to personal and school activities; 4. describe common things, events or experiences related to personal and daily activities; 5. convey an opinion about things and events in daily life; give a brief description about a phenomenon or a situation; 6. retell short stories.
	Reading	Can read common and simple textual materials related to daily and school life, get the gists and identify basic information. Can locate specific information in familiar materials, including: 1. read common and simple textual materials related to daily and school life, get the gists and identify basic information; 2. understand notes, messages, e-mails or short letters in social interactions; 3. understand brief introductions and descriptions in daily life; 4. understand predictable narrations and descriptions closely related to daily life and get the gists; 5. locate specific information in familiar materials.

16

Skills		Description of Objectives
Specific	Writing	Can use simple vocabulary to fill in forms with personal details or describe personal details. Can use basic vocabulary or sentences to communicate with others on familiar topics in writing. Can compose simple passages, including: 1. fill in forms and respond to questions with personal details or describe personal details; 2. use basic vocabulary or sentences to communicate with others on familiar topics in writing; 3. write short messages on familiar topics in social interactions; 4. record, copy or fill in forms with factual or expository information; 5. compose simple narrative or descriptive passages related to personal life, family life or campus life; 6. construct anecdotes or make simple plans.

3.4 Strategies

Strategies	Description of Objectives
Affective	1. understand motivation for learning a language; the aim of learning a language is to communicate with others and to express themselves; 2. resolve difficulties and seek help from others; 3. understand personal benefits of Chinese language learning, as well as for families and societies; 4. develop a positive attitude towards Chinese language, Chinese culture and other cultures; 5. be enthusiastically engaged in Chinese language learning and strive for expected results; 6. develop strategies for autonomous learning.

Strategies	Description of Objectives
Learning	1. develop critical thinking skills to obtain information; 2. develop memory by using body language; 3. learn to take notes and form a habit of note-taking; 4. identify the need to study and an interest in learning; 5. use isolated words to form complex descriptive sentences; 6. take notes on visual information and report in verbal information; 7. structure vertical progression; 8. accept constructive suggestions for revising their own work; 9. with teacher guidance, identify their own learning methods and learn to make a study plan; 10. with teacher guidance, make plans for further study; 11. engage in self-monitoring; 12. select learning methods most suited to the learners.
Communicative	1. with teacher guidance, communicate with teachers and classmates; 2. recognise linguistic barriers in communication and strive to overcome linguistic barriers; 3. use non-linguistic conventions (mime, gestures, etc.) to enhance the effectiveness of communication; 4. with teacher guidance, experience appropriate social etiquettes; 5. cooperate in group work.
Resource	1. with teacher guidance, learn to use textbooks, pictures, pictionaries, dictionaries, the Internet and multimedia resources to seek information; 2. learn to obtain language learning resources via teachers, classmates, friends, schools, communities and the workplace.
Interdisciplinary	1. expand one's personal knowledge base; 2. learn that the study of Chinese language and culture has given a fresh impetus to their learning of other subjects; 3. learn to relate the information obtained in other subjects to their learning of Chinese language and culture; with teacher guidance, use knowledge and skills acquired to assist in the learning of Chinese language and culture; 4. learn the importance of overall ability and with teacher guidance, develop their overall abilities; 5. this stage covers history, fine arts, folklore, etc.

3.5   Cultural Awareness

Awareness	Description of Objectives
Cultural Knowledge	1. know that individuals and communities have the right to learn different languages; 2. understand development and achievements in education and culture, locally and in China; 3. learn the history of Chinese culture and arts and their contributions to other cultures; 4. learn the history of Chinese language and culture and their contributions to other cultures; 5. know the essence of common Chinese sayings and proverbs, allusions and connotation; 6. know both linguistic and non-linguistic means of communication in Chinese culture; 7. know simple social etiquettes and customs in Chinese culture; 8. know social structure and interpersonal relations in Chinese culture; 9. learn Chinese people's contributions to their local society's prosperity.
Cultural Understanding	1. understand that culture is not only acquired, it is also learned via language; 2. know the relationships between culture and language learning, the latter being one important component of the former; 3. understand basic value-systems in Chinese culture; 4. come to experience cultural multiplicity, dynamics and permeability between cultures.
Cross-cultural Awareness	1. examine commonalities and differences between Chinese culture and their own culture; 2. learn the importance of cross-cultural awareness via learning about Chinese culture; 3. learn to view their own culture and ideology more objectively by engaging in comparisons between some elements of Chinese culture and their own.
Global Awareness	1. learn about other cultures and consider the importance of increased global perspectives via learning Chinese language; 2. begin to consider the importance of viewing the plurality of cultures from different perspectives via learning Chinese language and culture; 3. experience global citizenship.

Chapter Four　Stage 4 Objectives and Content

4.1　Objectives

Learners functioning within Stage 4 of ICCLE can understand language materials within sectors of social life. Can produce more correct sentences on familiar topics in description, explanation or comparison. Can compose simple passages or connect basic passages. Have demonstrated confidence and interest in learning the Chinese language. Have mastered some knowledge of learning strategies, communicative strategies, resource strategies and interdisciplinary strategies. Have gained introductory Chinese cultural knowledge and acquired preliminary cross-cultural awareness and international perspectives.

4.2　Linguistic Knowledge

Knowledge	Description of Objectives
Phonology	1. master sounds of *Pinyin* (Chinese Phonetic Alphabet, CPA); 2. understand discourses delivered in proper pronunciation, intonation and stress patterns; 3. produce correct tones and intonation patterns in everyday conversations; use correct liaison and tone changes; 4. produce correct and natural pronunciation and intonation in everyday conversations.
Character and Word	1. master 600 common Chinese characters (ideograms) toward proficiency in the four skills areas; 2. know conventions of character construction; 3. identify forms, sounds and meanings of Chinese characters; 4. know the patterns of Chinese words; 5. master 1,200 words related to society, daily life, workplace and campus life.
Grammar	Know and master: 1. adverbs of time; 2. particle 过 ; 3. complements of time and action; 4. the pattern of 是……的 ; 5. coverbal structures; 6. compound sentences.

Knowledge	Description of Objectives
Function	1. appropriately apply familiar communicative functions in different situations; 2. express temperament, attitudes or opinions effectively; 3. communicate with fluency and spontaneity in campus life, the workplace and social interactions.
Theme	1. explore topics on social life; 2. know topics related to customs and conventions, science, culture, literature and arts; 3. know contemporary news items about China and other countries.
Discourse	1. perceive differences and similarities in train of thought between Chinese language and learners' mother tongue; 2. learn to master the main stem of thought in sentences; understand connotations via modifiers and limiters; 3. try to apply simple and more complex rhetoric devices and recognise more complex rhetoric devices used in Chinese language; 4. learn temperament expressed in both spoken and written Chinese, based on features and functions of complex rhetoric devices.

21

4.3   Linguistic Skills

Skills	Description of Objectives
General	Can understand simple and familiar language materials closely related to workplace and social interactions and identify the main points and specific details. Can communicate with others on familiar topics with clarity and coherence and apply basic communicative strategies. Can develop increased effectiveness in communicating with others with the help of stresses, pauses, intonation or body language. Can narrate personal experiences, express personal views, and give simple reasons or explanations.

Skills		Description of Objectives
Specific	**Listening**	Can understand dialogues and speeches closely related to workplace and social activities; understand gists of statements or arguments and identify the main points and specific details, including: 1. understand dialogues and speeches related to workplace activities; identify main points and details; 2. understand gists and main information in dialogues and speeches related to social activities and grasp the intention of the speaker; 3. understand talks related to personal life or work; 4. understand gists of statements and arguments; 5. understand directions and requests related to general topics; 6. understand longer narrations.
	Speaking	Can communicate with others in the workplace or in social activities and take part in simple conversations or express personal views with clarity. Can maintain continuity, including: 1. can communicate with others on general topics in social activities; 2. take part in simple discussions and express personal opinions with clarity; 3. make suggestions or offer opinions on an issue and provide reasons; 4. use basic communicative strategies and express themselves clearly with maintained continuity; 5. process daily routines, give instructions and make arrangements; 6. narrate or report fairly thoroughly the process of an event.
	Reading	Can understand introductions, descriptions and narrations related to daily and school life, or the workplace; get the gists and locate key information, including: 1. read simple textual materials related to general contexts; get the gists and locate key information; 2. understand letters, e-mails, and notices related to workplace and social activities; 3. understand introductions and descriptions in daily life; 4. understand simple narrations and descriptions closely related to familiar topics; get the gists and locate specific details and understand the intention of the writer; 5. read factual texts and locate specific information.

Skills		Description of Objectives
Specific	**Writing**	Can describe daily activities in learning, work-related or social transactions, write short passages in a standard conventional format to convey or give adequate information, including: 1. take simple notes on reading or listening materials and summarise the main idea; 2. describe in coherent paragraphs familiar topics related to personal experiences, study, employment and social contacts; 3. fill in forms and make plans; 4. write simple notes on short oral presentations or reference materials; 5. compare and contrast alternatives; 6. keep diaries in coherent and correct sentences.

4.4   Strategies

Strategies	Description of Objectives
Affective	1. recognise the importance and significance of Chinese language learning; 2. encourage cooperation and be willing to share learning resources; 3. encourage perseverance among Chinese language learners and intention to overcome problems; 4. develop, adjust, and strengthen attitude and motivation in learning Chinese language; 5. develop positive affections towards Chinese language, Chinese culture and other cultures.
Learning	1. determine research topic and initiate inquiry; 2. keep a personal diary; 3. preview study content; 4. convert complex visual information to equally complicated verbal information; 5. structure both vertical and horizontal progression; 6. take an active part in tasks and activities; 7. create an environment to accept constructive suggestions for revising their own work; 8. with teacher guidance, make plans for further study and compensate for weaknesses.

Strategies	Description of Objectives
Communicative	1. use affective strategies to take part in classroom interactions with teacher guidance; 2. recognise linguistic barriers in communication and strive to overcome linguistic barriers; 3. communicate with others, including teachers and classmates both in and out of classrooms; 4. use non-linguistic conventions (mime, gestures, etc.) to enhance the effectiveness of communication; 5. observe social conventions in communication; 6. share success and failure in learning.
Resource	1. distinguish between fact and opinion when using a variety of sources of information; 2. use textbooks, pictures, pictionaries, dictionaries, the Internet, multimedia resources and newspapers to seek information; 3. obtain language learning resources via teachers, classmates, friends, schools, communities and the workplace.
Interdisciplinary	1. expand one's personal knowledge base; 2. learn that the study of Chinese language and culture has given a fresh impetus to their learning of other subjects; 3. learn to relate the information obtaind in other subjects to their learning of Chinese language and culture; with teacher guidance, use knowledge and skills acquired to assist in the learning of Chinese language and culture; 4. learn the importance of overall ability and develop their overall abilities; 5. this stage covers history, fine arts, folklores, geography, politics, economy and transportation.

4.5 Cultural Awareness

Awareness	Description of Objectives
Cultural Knowledge	1. know the right granted to members of a community to learn different languages; 2. know the right granted to members of a community or a society to use different languages; 3. understand development, communication and achievements in economy, culture, science and education locally and in China; 4. learn histories of Chinese literature, arts, science, and ideology, and their contributions to other cultures; 5. learn history of Chinese language and culture and their contributions to other cultures; 6. know the essence of common Chinese sayings and proverbs, allusion making and connotation; 7. know both linguistic and non-linguistic means of communication in Chinese language and culture; 8. know simple social etiquettes and customs in Chinese language and culture; 9. know social structure and interpersonal relationships in Chinese language and culture; 10. learn Chinese people's contributions to local society's prosperity.
Cultural Understanding	1. understand that culture is not only acquired, it is also learned via language; 2. know the relationships between culture and language learning, the latter being one important component of the former; 3. understand basic value-systems in Chinese culture; 4. come to experience cultural multiplicity, dynamics and permeability between cultures; 5. foster the foundations of critical thinking to learn and understand Chinese culture and local culture.

Awareness	Description of Objectives
Cross-cultural Awareness	1. examine commonalities and differences between Chinese culture and their own culture; 2. learn the importance of cross-cultural awareness via learning Chinese culture; 3. learn to view their own culture and ideology more objectively by engaging in comparisons between some elements of Chinese culture and their own.
Global Awareness	1. learn about other cultures and consider the importance of increased global perspectives via learning Chinese language; 2. begin to realize the importance of viewing the plurality of cultures from different angles via learning Chinese language and culture; 3. develop a sense of both national and international identity; 4. broaden their cultural horizons; 5. experience global citizenship.

Chapter Five　Stage 5 Objectives and Content

5.1　Objectives

Learners functioning within Stage 5 of ICCLE can understand a wide range of topics, produce correct sentences, write in paragraphs, create cohesive discourse, and express themselves fluently and spontaneously without much obvious searching for expressions. Have demonstrated confidence and a strong interest in learning the Chinese language. Have mastered knowledge with learning strategies, communicative strategies, resource strategies and interdisciplinary strategies. Have gained extensive Chinese cultural knowledge, and acquired preliminary cross-cultural awareness and international perspectives.

5.2　Linguistic Knowledge

Knowledge	Description of Objectives
Phonology	1. acquire clear and natural pronunciation and intonation in everyday communication; 2. express culture-specific connotations by means of pronunciation, intonation, and stress; 3. understand rhythm and melody in the Chinese language; 4. understand Putonghua (common speech) with a variety of accents.
Character and Word	1. master 800 common Chinese characters (ideograms) toward proficiency in the four skills areas; 2. know conventions of Chinese character construction; 3. apply forms, sounds and meanings of Chinese characters; 4. communicate with others or express themselves with appropriate words and phrases on familiar topics; 5. understand semantic change and neologisms in everyday life and apply 1,500 words.
Grammar	Know and master: 1. complements of result, of direction, of possibility and of degree; 2. 把 sentences; 3. passive voice; 4. compound sentences.

Knowledge	Description of Objectives
Function	1. apply familiar communicative functions in different situations appropriately; 2. learn and master new expressions and communicative functions as needed; 3. communicate with success in daily life, campus life and the workplace.
Theme	1. explore topics on social life; 2. apply previously acquired knowledge of topics.
Discourse	1. perceive differences and similarities in train of thought between Chinese language and learners' mother tongue; 2. learn to master the main stem of thought and understand connotations via modifiers and limiters; 3. master simple and more complex rhetoric devices and recognise ever more rhetoric devices used in Chinese language; 4. understand temperament expressed in both spoken and written Chinese, based on features and functions of complex rhetoric.

28

5.3　Linguistic Skills

Skills	Description of Objectives
General	Can understand more complex language materials closely related to a variety of occasions, including work-related and job-related ones, identify the main points and specific details, generalise and analyse. Can communicate with others using some communicative strategies, including discussions on general topics related to their occupation, personal viewpoints and attitudes, and seek suggestions. Can experience different accents and regional differences, and understand cultural significance of proverbs and idioms.

Skills		Description of Objectives
Specific	**Listening**	Can understand more complex dialogue and speech closely related to the workplace and specific field and identify the main points and basic facts; know the aims and intentions of the speaker, including: 1. understand more complex dialogue and speech related to workplace and social activities; 2. understand discussions and speeches related to work or professional field, identify main points and basic facts and grasp the viewpoints and arguments of the speaker; 3. understand more content of familiar topics, identifying main points and specific details; 4. understand simple explanations and narrations of a technical nature; 5. understand some proverbs, idioms, implications of and allusions to what is said; 6. understand Putonghua with a variety of accents on familiar topics.
	Speaking	Can engage in conversations on general topics, or in discussions or arguments, state reasons, express opinions and attitudes. Can engage in discussions on specific topics related to their employment or field, including: 1. communicate with others on general topics in most situations; 2. take part in description or present a position on interesting topics with clarity and continuity; 3. engage in more detailed conversations on specific topics; 4. join discussions and arguments, state their own opinions with clarity and argue with the conclusions of others.
	Reading	Can understand more complex language materials, determine main ideas, identify important facts and details and the structure of the text, including: 1. understand texts of descriptive material, get the gists, locate important facts and details and understand the structure of the text; 2. understand accurately narrative compositions containing some proverbs, idioms and figurative language; 3. understand introductions and descriptions with some new words and terms, get the gists and locate specific information; 4. understand simple popular science materials related to work, study or personal life.

Skills		Description of Objectives
Specific	Writing	Can describe, take notes, or explain on specific topics and write relevant documents or articles smoothly. Can reflect reality and express personal opinions, including: 1. communicate with others in writing on specific topics communicated in speech; 2. express personal views and opinions in coherent, smooth, and cohesive paragraphs; 3. describe in coherent paragraphs familiar topics related to personal experiences, study, employment and social contacts; 4. write simple notes on short oral presentations or verbal texts, write abstracts or brief reports; 5. write short articles, descriptive, narrative or explanatory in nature, on abstract or concrete topics, use appropriate vocabulary and coherent expressions, reflect reality and express their opinions with clarity.

5.4 Strategies

Strategies	Description of Objectives
Affective	1. understand and respect other people's feelings and emotions in Chinese language communication; 2. express in Chinese personal feelings, attitudes and value-systems; 3. increase and maintain motivation in learning Chinese language, strive to reach a higher level; 4. view from different perspectives the roles they play in the development of the world; 5. take part in activities which will help them to develop positive attitudes towards Chinese language and culture and to formulate good language learning habits.

Strategies	Description of Objectives
Learning	1. determine research on familiar topics and initiate inquiry; 2. identify main points in language learning; 3. organise and summarise their learning; 4. understand the value of learning Chinese language and develop an interest in self-learning; 5. convert complex visual information to equally complicated verbal information; 6. structure both vertical and horizontal progression; 7. create an environment to accept constructive suggestions from other people to overcome problems; 8. understand their own cognitive competencies and adjust their learning strategies to maximise the effectiveness of learning; accept responsibility for their own study, plan, monitoring, and assessment; 9. reflect on and examine their own objectives, progress, process, and adopted strategies.
Communicative	1. use affective strategies and take part in classroom interactions with teacher guidance; 2. overcome linguistic barriers in communication by repetition and clarification with teacher guidance; 3. communicate with ease both in and out of classrooms; 4. use non-linguistic conventions (mime, gestures, etc.) to enhance the effectiveness of communication; 5. observe social conventions in real communication situations; 6. share language learning experiences with one another.
Resource	1. distinguish between fact and opinion when using a variety of sources of information; 2. use proficiently textbooks, glossaries, dictionaries, newspapers and journals; seek information or obtain learning resources from libraries or the Internet.

31

Strategies	Description of Objectives
Interdisciplinary	1. expand one's personal knowledge base, build interdisciplinary readiness and be able to categorise; 2. apply proficiently what they have learned in other subjects to their learning of Chinese language and culture; 3. apply proficiently what they have learned in their learning of Chinese language and culture to the study of other subjects; 4. develop their overall abilities; 5. this stage covers history, fine arts, folklores, geography, politics, economy, transportation, literature and philosophy.

5.5   Cultural Awareness

Awareness	Description of Objectives
Cultural Knowledge	1. know the right granted to members of a community to learn different languages; 2. know the right granted to members of a community or a society to use different languages; 3. understand development, communication and achievements in economy, culture, science and education locally and in China; 4. learn China's achievements in literature, arts, science, and ideology, and their contributions to other cultures; 5. learn about the development of Chinese language and culture, and its contributions to and functions in other cultures; 6. know the essence of common Chinese sayings and proverbs, allusions and connotation; 7. know both linguistic and non-linguistic means of communication in Chinese language and culture; 8. know social etiquettes and customs of Chinese language and culture; 9. know social structure and interpersonal relations in Chinese language and culture; 10. understand fixed forms of the majority of cultural phenomena, which can be explained and interpreted in relation to another culture; 11. learn about the Chinese people's contributions to a local society's prosperity.

Awareness	Description of Objectives
Cultural Understanding	1. understand that culture is not only acquired, it is also learned via language; 2. know the relationships between culture and language learning, the latter being one important component of the former; 3. understand basic value-systems in Chinese culture; 4. understand cultural multiplicity, dynamics and permeability between cultures. 5. foster the foundations of critical thinking in learning and understanding Chinese culture and local culture.
Cross-cultural Awareness	1. examine commonalities and differences between Chinese culture and their own culture; 2. learn the importance of cross-cultural awareness via learning Chinese culture; 3. learn to view their own culture and ideology more objectively by engaging in comparisons between some elements of Chinese culture with their own.
Global Awareness	1. learn about other cultures and increase global perspectives via learning Chinese language; 2. understand Chinese cultural phenomena and their sources; 3. recognize the importance of interpreting the plurality of cultures from different perspectives through learning Chinese language and culture; 4. stimulate thinking and broaden their horizons via cultural studies; cultivate mediation caused by different cultural components; 5. understand Chinese culture and the local culture and their respective origins; 6. build strong global citizenship.

Appendix 1　Recommended Themes and Topics for Chinese Language Teaching

This table provides teachers and authors of CLT textbooks with a variety of themes and related information clues. The clues listed under each theme may overlap; therefore, users can make their choices according to specific needs. These themes and clues are applicable to all five stages and can be repeatedly used for different stages.

Themes	Recommended Topics
Personal Information	name, age, grade, birthplace, birthday, telephone number, address, contact information, family member, school life, working life, career, neighbor, language, hobby, education, hometown
Sentiments and Attitudes	like, dislike, happy, unhappy, agree, disagree, content, discontent, able, unable, likely, unlikely, complimentary, encouraging, thankful, regretful, revolted, resentful, anxious, humorous, trustful, doubtful, surprised, sad, sympathetic, fearful, worried, angry, complaining
Social Communication	greet, salute, exchange amenities, introduce, exchange business cards, extend thanks, bid goodbye, invite, refuse, visit, request, suggest, inform, allow, help, communicate, mediate, extend wishes and congratulations, go to parties, make appointments, go to dinner parties, make telephone calls, send e-mails, chat on line, customs and etiquettes, personal space, interpersonal relationships, appellations of family members, social titles, community life, donation and fund raising
Daily Life	daily life, school life, working life, make telephone calls, watch TV (news, weather reports), surf the Internet, do sports, health care, see doctors, ask directions, do housework, go shopping (price, size, shape, color), life necessities, eat out, dietary habits
School Life	knowledge, education, subjects, quality education, school titles, learning strategies, curriculum, scores, class language, rewards (scholarship, certificate of merit, commendation), discipline, go toschool, dismiss school, homework, activities (multicultural activities, after-class activities, school activities, community activities), school sports team, vacations, parents' meeting, school-opening ceremony, graduation ceremony, teacher-student relationship, make friends, school facilities, library

Appendix 1　Recommended Themes and Topics for Chinese Language Teaching

Themes	Recommended Topics
Family Life	marriage, family structure (dual-parent family, single-parent family), family members, appellations at home, communications between parents and children (generation gap), family activities, family plan, provide for the aged, family finance management, house trivias
Sports and Recreational Activities	sports events, international competition, regional competition, club sports, game, movie, TV programs, painting, music, dance, opera, drama, sports, weekend leisure, hobbies (reading, listening to music, collecting stamps)
Festivals	introductions of festivals, festivals of ethnical groups, cultural festivals, commemoration days of famous people, comparison of festivals
Health and Fitness	health (physical, mental), health consciousness, exercises, food, dietary habits, allergy-causing food, personal hygiene, traditional Chinese medicine, Western medicine, good life attitude, good interpersonal relationships, table manners, education and personal breeding, ideas about health
Customs and Taboos	age, income, marriage status, health, religious belief, political affiliation, colors and numbers with cultural connotations, private questions to be avoided in different cultures, taboos
Travel and Transportation	time, number, hotel, schedule, ask directions, map reading, traffic signpost, means of transportation, direction, distance, laws and regulations, unlawful behavior
Language and Culture	language learning strategies, benefits of language learning to the society and individuals, difficulties in language learning, links between language and culture, traditional ways of thinking, view the world from different angles, get a basic idea of the Chinese culture and enhance the understanding of one's own culture
Values	comparison of values, relationships between individual and the collective, authority and equality, competition and harmony, beauty and ugliness, thoughts and actions, moral norms

Themes	Recommended Topics
Literature and Arts	aesthetic conceptions, understand the mood and implication of art work, different genres of literary works (fiction, poem, essay, reportage, fairytale), different types of art works (music, chess, calligraphy, painting, photography, sculpture), appreciation of literary and art works from different countries
Politics, History and Geography	government structure of China, policies of China, diplomacy of China, laws of China, history of China, map of China, rivers of China, administrative division of China, surrounding countries of China
Science and Technology	science knowledge, science popularization, skill trainings
Globalization and Environment	globalization; one world, one family; environment conservation; pollution; use of resources; teaching of languages
Plan and Future	intention, plan, hope, wish
Hot Topics	global warming, natural disaster, refugee, pollution, drug, current affairs, surfing the Internet, war and peace
Education	moral education, intellectual education, physical education, aesthetic education, curriculum, textbooks, education system, education theories
Plants and Animals	flowers, grass, tree, various fruits, beasts and birds
Natural Phenomena	four seasons, weather (wind, cloud, thunder, lighting), river, lake, sea, hill, mountain, sun, moon, star, famous natural sceneries around the world

Appendix 2　CLT Subjects, Objectives and Sample Arrangements

The following tables are based on parts of the table in Appendix 1. Teachers can make changes to them according to their specific needs. Some words and expression listed in this Appendix are included in the *List of 800 Common Characters* or *List of 1500 Frequent Words*.

Personal Information

Subjects	Objectives	Sample Arrangements	Examples	Words
Name	can enquire people's names can tell others your own name can introduce others using their names	Group work: Ask students to introduce themselves by name. Then ask one of them to introduce the rest of the class by name.	1. 我叫小明。 2. 我姓王。 3. 我姓李。你呢? 4. 你叫什么名字? 5. 您贵姓?	姓，叫，姓名，名字，你，您，我，她，他，你们，我们，他们，中国，日本，美国，去年，今年，明年，男，女，男孩，女孩，说，
Birthplace	can enquire others' birthplaces using the right question sentence can correctly answer the question about your birthplace can correctly say the birthplace names of others'	Role-play in pairs: Divide students into pairs. Ask one student to tell the other his/her birthplace. The other makes a specific question about that place and tells the first student his/her own birthplace.	1. 我在中国出生。 2. 他在美国出生。 3. 你是在日本出生的吗? 4. 你/您（是）在哪里（国）出生的?	语言，英语，日语，法语，德语，阿拉伯语，西班牙语，意大利语，中国人，日本人，韩国人，英国人，澳洲人，美国人，德国人，法国人，加拿大人，意大利人，亚洲，欧洲，美洲，非洲，做，工作，什么，哪儿，哪个，

Subjects	Objectives	Sample Arrangements	Examples	Words
Nationality	can enquire others' nationalities can tell others your own nationality can list the languages you can speak	Give each student a card with a country name on it. Ask them to assume that they are from the country listed on the card. Then ask them to practice enquiring each other's nationality.	1. 你是哪国人？ 2. 我是中国人。 3. 你是法国人吗？ 4. 不是。我是意大利人。 5. 你会说什么语言？ 6. 我会说英语，也会说法语。	公司，医院，学校，商店，书店，邮局，银行，小学，中学，大学，学院，老师，职员，学生，警察，售货员，律师，医生，工程师，经理，司机，工人，也
Jobs	can enquire others' jobs can answer the question about your job with different sentence patterns	Ask students to ask and answer each other's questions about their or their family members' jobs.	1. 你做什么工作？ 2. 我是老师。 3. 你是老师吧？ 4. 是／不是。 5. 你妈妈在哪儿工作？ 6. 她在银行工作。	

38

Family and Friends

Subjects	Objectives	Sample Arrangements	Examples	Words
Appellation	can use the appellations for family members and relatives	1. ask students to bring photos of their families and introduce their family members to the class;	1. 我家有四口人，爸爸，妈妈，哥哥和我。 2. 姐姐比弟弟大三岁。 3. 哥哥是学生，妹妹也是学生。	爸爸，妈妈，哥哥，姐姐，弟弟，妹妹，儿子，女儿，爷爷，奶奶，姥姥（外婆），姥爷（外公），孙子，孙女，外孙子，

Appendix 2　CLT Subjects, Objectives and Sample Arrangements

Subjects	Objectives	Sample Arrangements	Examples	Words
Appellation		2. ask students to use the right Chinese appellations in introducing their family members.		外孙女，叔叔，妻子，丈夫，男朋友，女朋友，同学，同事，朋友，高，矮，胖，瘦，长，短，大，小，眉毛，眼睛，鼻子，嘴，耳朵，头发，头，脾气，性格，内向，外向，不爱说话，开朗，随和，急（躁），安静，聪明，勇敢，诚实，可靠，勤奋，认真，努力，能干，灵活，和蔼，骄傲
Relationships	can explain relationships between people can make simple comments on relationships between people	1. give specific situations to students and ask them to describe relationships between people; 2. ask students to describe someone they know and comment on their relationships.	1. 我们俩是好朋友。 2. 我们认识10年了。 3. 我们常常一起出国旅游。 4. 我们都喜欢乒乓球，（我们）经常在一起看比赛。	
Physical Features	can describe people's height and posture can make a simple account of others' clothing	1. show students some portrait photos and ask them to describe the physical features of the people;	1. 她长得很漂亮。 2. 他长得很帅。 3. 他很高。 4. 他常常穿一件蓝色的大衣。	

Subjects	Objectives	Sample Arrangements	Examples	Words
Physical Features	can describe people's facial features	2. describe the physical features of some students to the class and ask them to guess about who he/she is.	5. 她长头发，大眼睛，高高的鼻子。 6. 他戴着一副眼镜。	
Characters	can describe people's characters can tell the differences between people's characters can make simple comments on people's characters	1. ask students to look at some portrait photos and guess about people's characters; 2. give specific situations to students and ask them to compare and comment on people's characters.	1. 他比较外向。 2. 她比小王开朗／开朗多了。 3. 他的性格有点儿急。 4. 我的太太比较外向，而我比较内向。	

Home Life

Subjects	Objectives	Sample Arrangements	Examples	Words
Home	can describe the lay-out of houses	1. show students a picture and ask them to describe the lay-out of the house they see; 2. ask students to look at the picture and decorate the rooms in the house; 3. ask students to change the decoration style of the house in the picture. Then they must compare the new style with the old and find out the charac-teristics of each style;	1. 这是我的家。楼上有三间卧室，还有两间浴室。一层有一个大客厅，一个很大的厨房，一个饭厅和一个厕所。我特别喜欢客厅里的壁炉。书房在地下室，里面有很多书。客房也在地下室。地下室里可以打乒乓球，还可以健身，听音乐。我家虽然不太大，但是很舒适。 2. 这是一套三居室。 3. 这个房间朝阳。 4. 这栋公寓没有电梯。 5. 他的书房里到处都是书。 6. 公寓楼的水电费都很便宜。	客厅，卧室，书房，厨房，饭厅，厕所，洗手间，娱乐室，客房，车房，门，窗户，窗台，走廊，院子，楼梯，阳台，玻璃，衣柜，书柜，床，书桌，写字台，电视柜，沙发，餐桌，椅子，茶几，橱柜，灯，水龙头，喷头，锁，灶台，水池，窗帘，台布，床单，门帘，电视，响，音箱，录像机，DVD 机，录音机，VCD 机，洗碗机，热水器，烤箱，冰箱，微波炉，起床，刷牙，洗脸，早饭，午饭，晚饭，上班，下班，锻炼，睡觉，笤帚，拖布，抹布，洗洁精，吸尘器，

41

Subjects	Objectives	Sample Arrangements	Examples	Words
Home		4. ask students to think about elements to be considered for aged family members when moving house, e.g. it must be close to stores and bus stations, with a garden for flower planting.	7. 房租很贵。 8. 公寓楼和独栋房子相比就显得不大方便，停车比较 麻烦。	垃圾桶，垃圾袋，垃圾箱，牙膏，牙刷，毛巾，香皂，洗发水，洗发香波，浴液，好用，前面／边，后面／边，左面／边，右面／边，南面／边，北面／边，东面／边，西面／边，旁边，上面

Learning and Working

Subjects	Objectives	Sample Arrangements	Examples	Words
Learning Experiences	can enquire others' learning experiences can describe your own learning experiences	1. ask students to practice using different sentence patterns by enquiring each other's Chinese learning experiences, including time, place and contents; 2. describe your own learning experiences.	1. 你学了几年汉语了？ 2. 我学了三年汉语了，可是我说得不好。 3. 你学过中国音乐吗？ 4. 我（没）学过中国历史。 5. 汉字很难写。 6. 我已经学会两百多个汉字了。	汉语，英语，德语，法语，日语，韩语，西班牙语，阿拉伯语，写字，唱歌，提问题，复习，温习，工作，实习，打工，进修住，呆，生活，北京，上海，西门子，海尔，第一，第二，第几，

Subjects	Objectives	Sample Arrangements	Examples	Words
Working Experiences	can enquire others' working experiences can describe your own working experiences	1. enquire others' working experiences; 2. ask students to tell the class their own working experiences, including time, place, position and contents.	1. 我一边上学，一边工作。 2. 她已经工作两年了。 3. 你周末的时候打工吗? 4. 我现在读高二，周末经常去打工。 5. 你在哪儿工作? 6. 我在一家公司工作，是一名公司职员。 7. 我在北京工作三个月了。 8. 这是我的名片。	已经，这儿，那儿，这里，那里，这，那，半，小时，分钟，分，年，月，次，上次，每次，工人，经理，技术员，工程师，职员，经理，名片

43

Hobbies and Specialties

Subjects	Objectives	Sample Arrangements	Examples	Words
Hobbies	can ask and answer questions about hobbies	1. ask students to enquire each other's hobbies and specialties; 2. ask students to list hobbies and specialties of the famous people they know.	1.你有什么爱好? 2. 你喜欢什么运动? 3. 我爱／喜欢游泳。 4. 我最喜欢购物。 5. 他特别喜欢上网。 6. 我的爸爸喜欢打棒球。 7. 他弟弟特别喜欢踢足球。	游泳，旅游，上网，钓鱼，郊游，探险,骑自行车，爬山，散步，跑步，跳舞，体操，聊天，露营，做饭，健身运动，滑水，滑冰，购物，文学，书法，京剧，舞蹈，戏剧，看小说，电影，电视，戏，打，网球，乒乓球，篮球，排球，足球，羽毛球，板球，游戏，喝茶，听音乐，购物，逛商场
Specialties	can ask and answer questions about specialties		1.你有什么特长? 2. 他网球打得不错。 3. 他做中国菜很拿手。 4. 我不会打网球。	

Health and Fitness

Subjects	Objectives	Sample Arrangements	Examples	Words
Go to the Doctor's	can describe your symptoms can understand the doctor's simple questions and make answers	1. list some symptoms and ask students to name the related illnesses; 2. list names of some common diseases and ask students to role-play doctor and patient in pairs.	1. 你哪儿／哪里不舒服？ 2. 你怎么了？ 3. 我肚子疼得厉害。 4. 请你带我去医院好吗？ 5. 你发烧了，我觉得你应该去看医生。 6. 你脸色不太好，是不是（生）病了？ 7. 你的体温是多少？ 8. 我该去洗牙了。 9. 多休息，多喝水。 10. 嗓子有点儿炎症，吃点消炎药就好了。 11. 我的妈妈刚做了手术，很虚弱。	舒服，不舒服，感冒，生病，头疼，心脏病，肚子痛，癌症，糖尿病，肝炎，艾滋病，洗牙，洗手，医院，诊所，牙科医生，家庭医生，专科医生，手术，护士，急诊，外科，内科，妇科，儿科，老年，中年，青年，少年，幼儿，正常，血压高，血压低，药，开药，化验单，住院，健身，健身房，散步，打太极拳，游泳，爬山，跑步，打网球，

Subjects	Objectives	Sample Arrangements	Examples	Words
Do Exercises	can ask and answer questions about health can list exercises you do to keep fit	1. ask students to enquire each other's health; 2. ask students to tell others exercises they do to keep fit.	1. 你每天跑步吗? 2. 我和我的朋友天天慢跑 30 分钟。 3. 早睡早起身体好。 4. 你喜欢运动吗? 5. 你怎么锻炼身体? 6. 我每天早上打太极拳。	跳舞，练瑜伽，健美操，游泳馆，操场，跑步机，广场，运动场，中医，看中医，号脉，把脉，针灸，按摩，足疗，望，闻，问，切，中药，药材，中草药，抓药，脉，煎药，药方，汤药，丸药
Traditional Chinese Medicine	can understand instructions and diagnoses of the doctor can read directions of traditional Chinese medicines, with the help of a dictionary	1. ask two students to role-play doctor and patient; 2. ask students to find names of five traditional Chinese medicines in the library or on the Internet.	1. 请把舌头伸出来。 2. 先把这三服中药吃完，再来复查。 3. 你的面色发黄。 4. 这种药一天吃几片? 5. 你以前用过针灸吗?	

Food

Subjects	Objectives	Sample Arrangements	Examples	Words
Tableware and Cooking Utensils	can tell names of tableware and cooking utensils can describe the layout of a kitchen in China and one in your country	1. ask students to compete in picking up beans by chopsticks; 2. show students a picture of a Chinese- style kitchen. Ask them to list differences between it and those in their own countries.	1. 你会用筷子吗？ 2. 中国人一般不用刀叉吃饭。 3. 请给我一把勺子。 4. 烤箱里的鸡烤好了。 5. 炒菜好吃，但是油烟味儿比较大。	菜单，凉菜，热菜，主食，汤，家常菜，麻婆豆腐，青椒肉丝，北京烤鸭，西红柿鸡蛋汤，吃素，营养素，营养成分，维他命，维生素，矿物质，钙，铁，蛋白质，脂肪，能量，碳水化合物，含有，不能吃……（过敏），中餐，西餐，点心，日本料理，意大利菜，法国菜，风味，小吃，酸，甜，苦，辣，咸，油腻，清淡，好吃，生，熟，热，凉，点菜，结账，买单，打包，饿，饱，渴，服务员，小姐，
Food and Beverage	can talk and ask about food others like and dislike can ask and talk about daily diet	1. ask each student to make a list of groceries and compare their lists with each other; 2. ask students to list the most and least liked Chinese food in their countries and tell the class why. If necessary, the teacher can help them in their reports.	1. 你喜欢吃什么？ 2. 你吃米饭还是面条？ 3. 你吃过饺子吗？ 4. 我不爱喝咖啡。 5. 我吃了面包、小肉肠，还喝了杯牛奶。 6. 你们想喝什么饮料？ 7. 绿茶有益于身体健康。	

Subjects	Objectives	Sample Arrangements	Examples	Words
Eat Out	can read the menu and make an order from it can to ask about dishes you order can comment on the taste of food and drinks	1. ask students to make a Chinese menu (which includes cold dishes, hot dishes, staple food and their prices). Then ask them to role-play eating in a restaurant (make an order and pay the bill, etc.); 2. ask students to role-play the owner of a restaurant and make an advertisement for the restaurant.	1. 我们看一下儿菜单。 2. 今天有什么特别推荐的菜，请你介绍一下儿。 3. 想吃点儿什么？ 4. 我喜欢海鲜。 5. 我想点一道法国菜。 6. 中国的火锅很有特色。 7. 这个菜是用什么做的？ 8. 结账（买单）！	服务生，烹调，炒，煎，烧，煮，炖，烤，蒸，筷子，盘子，刀，叉，锅，碗，杯子，汤匙勺，烤肉，牛排，小羊排，炖牛肉，香肠，沙拉，番茄酱，盐，胡椒，饮料，汽水，可乐，果汁，咖啡，茶，雪碧
Dietary Habits	can get acquainted with the basic cooking methods can talk and ask about personal dietary habits can talk and ask about dietary habits of people in your own country and other countries	1. prepare a Chinese dish and ask students to have a taste and make comments; 2. ask students to role-play journalist and interview each other on their dietary habits (e.g. Can you eat spicy food?). Then ask them to report the results.	1. 日本菜有什么特点？ 2. 日本人常吃生的菜。 3. 中国菜有点儿油腻。 4. 今天我们准备了烤肉和沙拉。 5. 我喜欢清淡点儿的菜。 6. 我不吃辣的。 7. 我们常吃鱼。 8. 太咸了！	

Shopping

Subjects	Objectives	Sample Arrangements	Examples	Words
Currency	can say names of commonly used currencies can recognize RMB of different face values can say the amount of money	1. show pictures of RMB to students and ask them to tell you the face values; 2. show price tags to students and ask them to tell you the sums.	25.80 元—— 二十五块／元 八毛 102.38 元—— 一百零二元三角八分	人民币，美元，欧元，日元，英镑，元（块），角（毛），分，公斤，斤，两，磅，千克，水果，苹果，梨，香蕉，西瓜，草莓，桔子，葡萄，桃，服装，上衣，裤子，西装，裙子，衬衫，T恤，鞋，帽子，袜子，件，条，双，套，个，张，台，罐，包，瓶，盒，大号，中号，小号，米，公分，尺，寸，大，小，长，短，肥，瘦，便宜，贵，打折，多少，钱，零钱，信用卡，收银台，收据，红，绿，蓝，黄，黑，
Unit and Size	can name the commonly seen goods and commonly used classifiers can say models and sizes of goods	1. name the commonly seen goods; 2. ask students to make a shopping list.	一条裙子 两双袜子 一斤苹果 一袋米	
Price	can tell others your demands can ask and answer questions about prices can bargain on prices	1. show price tags to students and ask them to answer questions about prices; 2. give cards to students and ask them to role play customer and vendor.	1. 我要一杯咖啡。 2. 我买一本书。 3. 可以试试吗？ 4. 这个多少钱？ 5. 苹果多少钱一斤？ 6. 这个有点儿贵，能便宜点儿吗？ 7. 可以打折吗？	

49

Subjects	Objectives	Sample Arrangements	Examples	Words
Price	can use sentences for making payment	According to information on the cards, they should include making request, asking for price, bargaining and making payment in their conversations.	8. 我买两个，能便宜点儿吗？ 9. 给您钱。 10. 找您五块钱。 11. 能用信用卡吗？	白，灰，棕，金色，深（蓝等），纯，棉，毛，丝，麻，玻璃，金，银，木，好，坏，真，假，退，换
Material and Quality	can say different colours can say different materials can make simple comment on goods	1. show pictures to students and ask them to tell the colours, materials of these goods and make comments on them; 2. ask students to list items in the class room or their home and describe the colours, materials and qualities of these things.	1. 我要买一辆红色的车。 2. 这件衬衫是纯棉的。 3. 太贵了。 4. 太长了。 5. 挺时髦的。	
Return and Replace Goods	can raise one's demands can state reasons	Ask students to demand refunding or replacing the goods, according to reasons listed on the cards (e.g. improper colour, poor quality, wrong size) given to them.	1. 这个能退吗？ 2. 可以换一个吗？ 3. 这种颜色不适合我。	

50

Bank

Subjects	Objectives	Sample Arrangements	Examples	Words
Open an Account	can open an account in a Chinese bank	1. ask students to fill out the form needed for opening an account; 2. ask students to role-play opening an account in a bank.	1. 我要开一个账户。 2. 请把这张单子填一下儿。 3. 活期的还是定期的? 4. 我要兑换一点儿外汇。	储蓄，付款，支票，汇款，存折，定期，活期，股票，退休金，账号，账户，户头，填表，手续费，储蓄卡，身份证，美元，英镑，欧元，日元，人民币，零钱，整钱，纸币，硬币，面额，面值，兑换，汇率，收据，投资
Deposit and Withdraw Accounts	can make clear the amount of money you want to deposit or withdraw	1. ask students to fill out a deposit form of RMB; 2. ask students to fill out a form of withdrawal and role-play customer and bank clerk.	1. 我要存 2000 元人民币。 2. 我想取 1000 美元。 3. 自动取款机在哪儿? 4. 请输入密码。 5. 我可以直接取美元吗? 6. 我不会填写取款单。	
Change Money	can make clear the amount of RMB you want to change	1. ask each student to play the role of a bank clerk. The rest of the class go to him/her to change the money of their own countries into RMB (for international class);	1. 您要换多少? 2. 我想换 1000 欧元。 3. 换成人民币。 4. 我想把这张纸币换成硬币。 5. 今天的汇率是多少?	

Subjects	Objectives	Sample Arrangements	Examples	Words
Change Money	can make clear the amount of changes you need	2. ask two students to role-play customer and bank clerk, changing a 100-*yuan* note into one 50-*yuan* note, two 20-*yuan* notes and two 5-*yuan* notes.	6. 请拿好。 7. 我想把美元换成人民币。 8. 请把这张单子填好。	

Travel and Transportation

Subjects	Objectives	Sample Arrangements	Examples	Words
Ask Directions	can ask directions and understand the direction given by others can show directions to others	1. say a place name and students should ask directions to get there and the first to arrive is the winner; 2. give two maps (A and B) to students and the one with Map B must ask the one with Map A for directions because the way is shown only on Map A. Then the two students exchange maps and their roles.	1. 请问，去北京大学怎么走？ 2. 附近有没有银行？ 3. 往前走，到红绿灯向右拐。 4. 要走多长时间？ 5. 往前走 100 米就到了。 6. 得坐车吗？ 7. 还是打车去吧。 8. 过了马路就到了。	走，坐车，往，拐，转，米，公尺，公里，对面，旁边，附近，红绿灯，路口，十字路口，远，近，楼上，楼下，前，后，左，右，东，西，南，北，交通工具，公共汽车，巴士，地铁，轮船，火车，飞机，汽车，自行车，出租车，长途车，走路，换

Subjects	Objectives	Sample Arrangements	Examples	Words
Traffic Vehicles	can know how to take the common means of public transportation, i.e. buses, subways and taxis can know how to take the train and airplane in China	1. ask students to role-play bus conductor and passenger, using the most commonly used sentences; 2. divide the class into two groups and ask them to debate on "Which is better, ride a bicycle or drive a car?" Each group should state their supporting reasons and list the advantages and disadvantages of using the two vehicles.	1. 到故宫坐几路车? 2. 在哪儿倒／换车? 3. 一张颐和园。 4. 这个位子有没有人坐? 5. 下车。 6. 劳驾。 7. 飞机就要起飞（降落）了。 8. 去人民大会堂。	（倒）车，买票，上，下，座位，售票员，查票员，软卧，硬卧，硬座，检票，订票，经济舱，航班，航空公司，转机，单程，往返，登机，行李，托运，安检，机场班车，车站，机场，售票处，站台，车厢，登机口，候车（机）室，列车员，司机，乘客，空姐，出发，到达，起飞，正点，准点，晚点，预订，安排，旅馆，房间，单人间，双人间，房间号，钥匙，洗
Make Reservations	can book airplane tickets and train tickets can book rooms in a hotel	1. ask students to read flight names and role-play making telephone calls to book a seat;	1. 我要预订一张去上海的机票。 2. 有今天下午去西安的经济舱吗? 多少钱? 3. 我要预订一个双人间，住两晚。	

Subjects	Objectives	Sample Arrangements	Examples	Words
Make Reservations		2. ask students to role-play calling a hotel, asking about the rooms (quite or not, smoking or non-smoking, facilities, etc.) and making a reservation.	4. 带洗澡间吗？含早餐吗？ 5. 我已经预订了一个双人间。 6. 有空房间吗？ 7. 请填一下儿住宿登记卡。 8. 我要退房了，请结账。	澡间，卫生间，厕所，餐厅，前台，服务，打扫，叫醒，送餐，洗衣，请勿打扰，手续，入住，退房，结账，现金，信用卡，旅行支票，免税，个人物品，报关，护照，入境，出境，海关，检查，（填写）申报单，登记卡，签证，护照，国籍
Go Through Formalities	can check in and out of hotels can go through Customs formalities	1. divide the class into pairs. Ask them to role-play checking in and out at the reception desk of a hotel; 2. ask students to rol-play going through Customs.	1. 请填一下儿海关申报单（入境登记卡）。 2. 请出示您的护照。 3. 请把包里的东西都拿出来。 4. 这张画不能带出境。	

54

Appendix 2 CLT Subjects, Objectives and Sample Arrangements

Subjects	Objectives	Sample Arrangements	Examples	Words
Hotel Services	can ask for some services	1. ask students to role-play guest and hotel clerk. The guest should ask for some services (ordering food, morning call, laundry, etc.); 2. ask students to role-play guest and hotel clerk. The guest is complaining about the poor services.	1. 请明早 6 点叫醒我。 2. 我需要客房服务。 3. 我房间的空调坏了。 4. 请把这个包拿到 808 房间。	

Attitudes and Sentiments

Subjects	Objectives	Sample Arrangements	Examples	Words
Like	can express your likes	Prepare cards with smilies and cards with activities. Ask students to draw a card from each group and describe what's on each card. One smily means they like the activity. Two smilies mean they quite like the activity. Three smilies mean they like the activity very much.	1. 你喜欢这本书吗? 2. 我非常喜欢这本书。 3. 我对跳舞非常感兴趣。 4. 她特别爱听京剧。 5. 你喜欢不喜欢这本书? 6. 我特别喜欢二胡。	很，非常，太，特别，喜欢，爱，兴趣，怎么样，好吗，行吗，好，行，好的，可以，同意，没问题，对不起，抱歉，想，要，能，可以，觉得，认为，但是，可是，建议，意见，看法，

Subjects	Objectives	Sample Arrangements	Examples	Words
Dislike	can express your dislikes	Game: Prepare some activity cards and show the pictures to students and then stick them on the blackboard with the reverse side to the whole class. Divide the whole class into two groups and ask each group to send a student to the front of the classroom. The rest of the two groups should use different sentence patterns to express dislikes of these activities. The two students in the front should find the card with the activities mentioned by their group. A correct finding gains each group a mark. The group with the higher score wins the game.	1. 我不爱看电影。 2. 我对电视不感兴趣。 3. 你觉得这部电影怎么样？ 4. 我不太喜欢喝茶。 5. 我不喜欢暴力电影。 6. 我不喜欢跑步，但我喜欢打球。 7. 我不喜欢小狗，我喜欢大狗。 8. 我不喜欢打听别人的私事，也不爱听。 9. 我不喜欢骂人。	想法，打算，说好，办法，同意，不同意，反对，不行，不可以，不可能

Appendix 2　CLT Subjects, Objectives and Sample Arrangements

Subjects	Objectives	Sample Arrangements	Examples	Words
Agree	can show you agree with others in a proper way	Game: Say some sentences to the whole class and ask them to make quick judgements. If the sentence expresses a normal situation (e.g. Let's speak Chinese.), students should agree. If it's a wrong statement (e.g. It's midnight now.), students should disagree. Those who make the wrong judgements are out. Those who can hold on to the end are winners of the game.	1. 我没有意见。 2. 我同意你的看法。 3. 你的建议不错。 4. 你说的一点儿都不错。 5. 我也是这么想的。 6. 我们一起去书店怎么样？ 7. 好／好的。 8. 我们去听中国文化讲座，好不好？ 9. 我答应李伟明天下午一起去看电影。	
Disagree	can show you disagree with others in a proper way	Debate: Divide students into two groups. One group supports the opinion listed on the card, while the other shows disagreement using different sentence patterns.	1. 我不同意你的意见。 2. 这种说法不对。 3. 他的说法太可笑了。 4. 这种说法有问题。 5. 这种观点不正确。 6. 你的意见我同意是同意，不过还有些问题需要考虑。	

Plans

Subjects	Objectives	Sample Arrangements	Examples	Words
Plans	can ask and answer questions about time and date can ask and answer questions about plans	1. ask students to tell the time shown on clocks or watches; 2. ask students to tell the date shown on the calendar; 3. ask students to list birthdays of their relatives and friends; 4. ask students to make plans for holidays; 5. ask students to make schedules for a day in their life.	1. 现在几点了？ 2. 现在两点半。 3. 你的生日是几月几号？ 4. 我的生日是6月8号。 5. 今天星期几？ 6. 今天星期三。 7. 这个周末你打算/准备做什么？ 8. 我想/要/打算去天安门。 9. 几点了？	点，分（钟），秒，半，一刻，差，年，月，日，星期，礼拜，打算，计划，准备，要，想，周末，夏天，暑假，春天，寒假，圣诞节，感恩节，宗教节日，新年，春节，中秋节，端午节，黄金周，长假

58

Social Communication

Subjects	Objectives	Sample Arrangements	Examples	Words
Make Requests	can make requests can make requirements in a tactful way	1. ask students to make requests to each other; 2. ask students to mimic the situation of proposing.	1. 劳驾，请把那本词典递给我。 2. 把奶油递给我好吗？谢谢。 3. 拜托了。 4. 你能帮我个忙吗？	劳驾，请，求，可以，建议，怎么样，帮忙，帮助

Appendix 2   CLT Subjects, Objectives and Sample Arrangements

Subjects	Objectives	Sample Arrangements	Examples	Words
Make Requests			5. 你愿意跟我结婚吗？ 6. 你愿意做我的女朋友吗？	
Make Suggestions	can ask for suggestions can make suggestions can make suggestions in a tactful way	1. ask students to ask for or make suggestions in different situations; 2. ask students to make suggestions in a tactful way.	1. 我的建议如何？ 2. 你有什么建议？ 3. 我希望我们周末能一起去游泳。 4. 周末我们去长城，好吗？	

59

Climate

Subjects	Objectives	Sample Arrangements	Examples	Words
Seasons	can name the four seasons in Chinese and your mother tongue can tell differences of the four seasons	1. show students pictures of the four seasons and ask them to identify the seasons and list the characteristics of each season; 2. divide the whole class into pairs and ask students to tell partners climate changes in their hometown.	1. 一年有几个季节？ 2. 你最喜欢什么季节？ 3. 这里春天很温暖，夏天很炎热，秋天很凉快，冬天很寒冷。 4. 北京的春天怎么样？ 5. 北京一年四季分明。	雾，阳光，风，雷，闪电，雷阵雨，潮湿，干燥，暖和，热，桑拿天，凉快，冷，降温，晴朗，阴天，多云，晴转阴，晴转多云，大风，刮风，（下）雨，（下）雪，季节，气候，四季，春天，夏天，

Subjects	Objectives	Sample Arrangements	Examples	Words
Seasons		Each student should note down the climate characteristics of the other's city and report to the whole class.	6. 这里冬季寒冷干燥，夏季高温多雨。 7. 哈尔滨冬天的最低气温能达到零下40°C。 8. 北京的秋天最好。 9. 我最怕热!	秋天，冬天，旱季，雨季，很，非常，特别，极了，够，挺，最，温度，气温，升高，降低，保暖，防寒，摄氏度，天气预报，播送，地区，零下，白天，夜间，四季分明，大风降温
Climate Characteristics	can use words and terms about climate (cold, hot, cool, warm, etc.) can understand weather terms can tell differences in climate between different places	1. show students pictures of different weather conditions and ask them to name the conditions; 2. show a map to students and ask them to listen to the weather forecast recording, mark the weather conditions on the cities, and report to the whole class;	1. 明天天气怎么样? 2. 今天天气真好。 3. 今天可能会下雨，出门要带雨伞。 4. 今天真够热的。 5. 秋天到了，天气越来越凉快了。 6. 今天的最高气温只有5°C。 7. 今天的气温比昨天高3°C。	

60

Appendix 2 CLT Subjects, Objectives and Sample Arrangements

Subjects	Objectives	Sample Arrangements	Examples	Words
Climate Characteristics		3. ask students to tell the differences between the climate of their hometown and that of Harbin, Beijing or Guangzhou.	8. 海南比北京热多了。 9. 上海没有北京冷。 10. 今天有五级风。 11. 雪越下越大。 12. 南方和北方温差很大。 13. 家家户户都关心全球气候的变暖。	

Nature

Subjects	Objectives	Sample Arrangements	Examples	Words
Plants	can name the commonly seen plants can make simple introductions on the characteristics of plants can make a brief account of functions of plants	1. show pictures of plants to students and ask them to read names of these plants; 2. ask students to list three commonly seen plants and briefly introduce their characteristics and functions, or make a brief comment on them.	1. 这朵花真香。 2. 迎春花在春天开。 3. 竹子的中间是空的。 4. 牡丹花真漂亮。 5. 今年葡萄长得很好。 6. 植树造林对保护环境有好处。 7. 很多植物都可以作为药材。	树，草，森林，绿化，松树，杨树，柳树，竹子，苹果树，柿子树，枣树，花，玫瑰，牡丹，菊花，兰花，梅花，勿忘我，迎春花，康乃馨，野花，粮食，小麦，大米，白薯，花生，玉米，大豆，土豆，马铃薯，

Subjects	Objectives	Sample Arrangements	Examples	Words
Animals	can name the commonly seen animals can make simple introductions on the habits of commonly seen animals	1. ask students to list names of the 12 symbolic animals in the Chinese zodiac system; 2. ask students to tell the class one of their favourite animals.	1. 熊猫喜欢吃竹叶。 2. 狗会看家。 3. 除了熊猫，别的动物我都不太喜欢。 4. 金鱼不好养。 5. 我养的小鸟很可爱。	燕麦，种，种植，种地，养，植物，药材，狗，猫，牛，马，羊，鸡，猪，鸭子，鸟，猴子，老虎，兔子，蛇，狮子，大象，熊猫，肉食动物，食草动物，宇宙，银河系，太阳系，太阳，水星，金星，木星，火星，土星，天王星，海王星，冥王星，地球，月亮，公转，自转，大爆炸，黑洞，彗星，行星，恒星，卫星，地震，海啸，火山，喷发，洪水，飓风，
Celestial Bodies	can name important celestial bodies can get basic knowledge about celestial bodies	1. show students pictures of celestial bodies and ask them to tell their names; 2. ask students to tell the class what they know about celestial bodies;	1. 月亮是地球的卫星。 2. 太阳是一颗恒星。 3. 月亮本身不发光。	

Subjects	Objectives	Sample Arrangements	Examples	Words
Natural Disasters	can name natural disasters	1. show students pictures of natural disasters and ask students to name them; 2. show students pictures of natural disasters and ask them to explain the causes and results and list preventive measures. 3. ask students to surf the Internet for information about natural disasters.	1. 这次地震的震中在太平洋海底。 2. 这次海啸是由地震引起的。 3. 这次水灾造成3000多人死亡。 4. 除了人员伤亡外，这次火灾还造成了巨大的财产损失。	冰雹，水灾，火灾，旱灾，虫灾，难民，灭火器

Language Learning

Subjects	Objectives	Sample Arrangements	Examples	Words
Problems in Language Learning	can ask questions when having problems can make clear your problems in learning Chinese and state the reasons	1. ask students to list their problems in learning Chinese; 2. ask students to list their own solutions in learning Chinese.	1. 这个字／词用汉语怎么说？ 2. 我的发音不太好。 3. 声调不对。 4. 汉语发音不太难。 5. 汉字很难写，可是非常有意思。 6. 请你再说一遍。 7. 请你说慢／清楚一点儿。	拼音，读音，声调，声母，韵母，元音，辅音，儿化，四声，发音，汉字，偏旁，部首，笔画，笔顺，多音字，简体字，繁体字，词类，

Subjects	Objectives	Sample Arrangements	Examples	Words
Language Learning Strategies	can understand strategies of others can tell others your own learning methods	1. list some commonly used learning methods on the blackboard and ask students to choose the one(s) they use; 2. divide students into pairs and ask them share their learning methods with each other.	1. 上课之前先预习。 2. 大声朗读生词／课文。 3. 每天课后要复习。 4. 经常看生词表。 5. 经常和中国人聊天。 6. 每天早上听15分钟的汉语录音。 7. 每天读一篇汉语文章。 8. 制订一个学习计划表。 9. 认真完成作业。	名词，动词，形容词，副词，连词，助词，叹词，介词，汉语，方言，书面语，外来语，术语，例句，搭配，复习，聊天，听录音，看生词，读，提问，上网，学习，作业，抄写，毛笔字，朗读，清晰，清楚，准确
Chinese Characters	can identify and distinguish basic radicals of Chinese characters	1. divide the whole class into two groups. Give each group pictographic and phonetic elements of the same 20 commonly used Chinese characters. Each group have two minutes to prepare. Then ask them to match	1. 这个字是多音字。 2. 这个字怎么读? 3. 这个汉字的笔画很多。 4. 这是个左右结构的汉字。 5. 这个偏旁的意思是水。 6. 我们没学过这个字。	

Subjects	Objectives	Sample Arrangements	Examples	Words
Chinese Characters		these elements to form Chinese characters and write their *Pinyin*; 2. write a story on the blackboard, leaving some Chinese characters' strokes missing and ask students to point them out and make corrections.	7. 汉字太有趣了! 8. 他很聪明，汉字一学就会了。	

Literature and Arts

Subjects	Objectives	Sample Arrangements	Examples	Words
Literature and Arts	can tell the main literature genres can tell the main forms of arts	1. ask students to make a brief introduction on the literature and art works they know; 2. show students pictures of art works and ask them details of these works, such as names, artists and main images.	1. 你喜欢中国诗词吗? 2. 你看过《西游记》吗? 3. 诗歌是中国唐朝的主要文学形式。 4. 明清时期中国小说很繁荣。 5. 他书架上的书不是中国古典小说就是外国名著。	诗歌，散文，小说，雕塑，摄影，绘画，戏剧，周（朝），唐（朝），宋（朝），元（朝），明（朝），清（朝），《诗经》，《红楼梦》，《三国演义》，《水浒传》，《西游记》，《狂人日

Subjects	Objectives	Sample Arrangements	Examples	Words
Famous Literary Figures and Works	can get a basic idea of famous Chinese writers and their works can get a basic idea of famous Chinese artists and their works		1. 你能介绍一下儿唐朝诗人李白的情况吗？ 2. 《西游记》是一部有名的中国古典小说。 3. 只要提起唐朝诗人，人们就会想到李白。 4. 只有杜甫才称得上是"诗圣"。	记》，《家》，李白，杜甫，陆游，曹雪芹，罗贯中，施耐庵，吴承恩，鲁迅，巴金，老舍，丁西林，孙悟空，唐僧，诸葛亮，刘备，曹操，宋江，林冲，贾宝玉，林黛玉
Classical Images	can get a basic idea of the classical images in literature can get a basic idea of the classical images in other art forms		1. 林黛玉是哪部小说中的人物？ 2. 阿Q是一个什么样的人物？ 3. 在中国，不管大人还是小孩儿，都知道孙悟空。	

History and Geography

Subjects	Objectives	Sample Arrangements	Examples	Words
Historical Figures	can name some famous figures in the history of China and tell the stories of them	Show students photos of some famous people in the history of China. Write their names on small cards and hand them out to students. Ask them to stick these cards to the right photos.	1. 你知道毛泽东吗? 2. 秦始皇是中国历史上的第一位皇帝。 3. 孔子是中国伟大的思想家。 4. 孔子不但是伟大的思想家，而且还是伟大的教育家。	历史，朝代，公元，公元前，中世纪，孔子，秦始皇，李白，成吉思汗，毛泽东，郑和，丝绸之路，新中国成立，世界，亚洲，欧洲，非洲，美洲，大洋洲，国家，首都，人口，省，市，自治区，直辖市，特别行政区，县，州，省会，首府，平原，高原，山地，盆地，草原，森林，沙漠，海湾，河流，湖，江，林业，农业，
Historical Events	can tell some famous events in the history of China can tell famous historical events in the history of your own country	Ask each student to write a short introduction for a picture they like most (picture of historical figures, sites, or events). Each student should show the picture to the whole class and make a short presentation before sticking it on the wall.	1. 丝绸之路是从西安开始的。 2. 你听说过"郑和下西洋"的故事吗? 3. 你知道中华人民共和国是什么时候成立的吗? 4. 历史与其说是伟人创造的，还不如说是人民创造的。	

Subjects	Objectives	Sample Arrangements	Examples	Words
Historical Events			5. 屈原宁可投江自尽，也不愿苟且偷生。	工业，旅游业，商业，铁矿，煤矿，石油，木材，出产，进出口，制造，电子产品，生产
Geography	can locate China on the map and name China's capital and capital cities of all provinces can name the main neighbouring countries of China can name your own country, its capital, all the states/provinces and the main cities can tell the population of China can tell the general situation of industries in your country	Divide the whole class into pairs. One student names a province and the other looks for it on the map. Each student has 10 chances.	1. 中国的首都是北京。 2. 我家在美国的华盛顿州。 3. 中国有 13.6 亿人，是世界上人口最多的国家。 4. 中国的西部有高原。 5. 中国是一个地大物博、人口众多的国家。	

Religions and Folk Customs

Subjects	Objectives	Sample Arrangements	Examples	Words
Religions	can get acquainted with the main religions in China can get some idea of the main religions of the world can tell others your own religious belief and religious activities you often attend	Show students pictures about different religions (church, temple, mosque, famous religious figures) and ask them to make descriptions.	1. 这是北京最大的清真寺。 2. 我们一家人都信天主教。 3. 佛教大约是在公元 1 世纪时传到中国来的。	佛教，基督教，天主教，伊斯兰教，印度教，宗教，教堂，牧师，神父，礼拜，聚会，祈祷，圣诞节，复活节，斋戒，朝圣，佛堂，烧香，寺庙，皈依，吃斋，念佛
Folk Customs and Culture	can gain some knowledge of Chinese folk customs, idioms and famous Chinese people around the world	Tell students a Chinese myth or folklore and ask them to repeat it.	1. 龙是中华民族的象征。 2. 旗袍不仅是中国的，也是世界的。 3. 中国民间有一个传统习俗，过春节的时候，全家团圆，一起吃年夜饭。 4. 红色在中国传统文化中表示大吉大利。	

69

Appendix 3　Subjects and Learning Objectives on Chinese Culture

The following table provides a number of cultural subjects for users to develop on according to their needs. Most of the subjects are applicable to all five stages, and can be used repeatedly in different stages where necessary.

Stage 1 Cultural Subjects and Learning Objectives

Subjects	Learning Objectives	Sample Questions on Cross-cultural Communication
Customs and Etiquettes	1. to learn the basic Chinese terms of greeting when two persons meet: apart from *nihao* 你好 (How are you?), the other commonly used terms of greeting include *ninhao* 您好 (How are you?) *chifan le ma* 吃饭了吗？"(Have you had your meal?) and *qu nar* 去哪儿？(Where are you going?); 2. to gain some idea about the cultural connotations the Chinese attach to colors. For instance, red suggests happiness and festivity;	1) What are the etiquettes when you greet people in your country? How are they different from the Chinese? 2) Which color suggests happiness and festivity in your country? Does the color red mean anything to you in your cultural tradition?

Appendix 3   Subjects and Learning Objectives on Chinese Culture

Subjects	Learning Objectives	Sample Questions on Cross-cultural Communication
Customs and Etiquettes	3. to gain some idea about the cultural connotations the Chinese attach to numbers. For instance, the number 6 conveys the meaning of smoothness, the number 8 implies wealth because it is homophonic with *fa* 发, meaning "affluence"; by the same token, the number 9 suggests longevity; and the Chinese dislike the number 4 because it carries the disagreeable undertone of *si* 死, which means "death".	3) Are there any taboos pertaining to numbers in your country? Which numbers are adored, and which numbers are disliked in your country? Why?
Appellation	1. to understand and master the Chinese way of appellation: the surname comes before the given name; the surname is often followed by such titles as *laoshi* 老师 (teacher), *xiansheng* 先生 (sir), *nüshi* 女士 (lady) and *taitai* 太太 (madam). A surname or given name consists of one or two Chinese characters; 2. to gain some general knowledge of the Chinese notion of family. The Chinese people value their family relationship highly, and generally avoid addressing their parents, siblings and other family members directly by their names.	1) Is the way of appellation in your country the same as that in China? If not, what are the differences? 2) Are children in your country allowed to call their parents directly by their names? How do you address each other in your family?

Subjects	Learning Objectives	Sample Questions on Cross-cultural Communication
Chinese Animal Signs	1. to be acquainted with the names of the 12 symbolic animals in the Chinese zodiac system and remember their correct sequence, i.e. rat, ox, tiger, rabbit, dragon, snake, horse, sheep, monkey, rooster, dog, and pig; to know their corresponding relationships with the Gregorian calendar; and to single out which one of these animals represents your year of birth; 2. to learn the legends related to the 12 symbolic animals in the Chinese zodiac system. For instance, why rat comes on top of the list?	1) Are there any methods of age computation in your country akin to the Chinese animal signs? 2) If yes, what are their similarities to and differences from the Chinese way? 3) Do people in your country use a set of 12 constellation figures? If yes, how different is your set from the Chinese one? 4) Are there any legends in your country that are similar to those about the Chinese animal signs?

72

Stage 2 Cultural Subjects and Learning Objectives

Subjects	Learning Objectives	Sample Questions on Cross-cultural Communication
Music, Dance and Painting	1. to acquire a fundamental knowledge of China's unique music and its basic classifications, i.e. classical music, folk music and popular music; to be acquainted with the most commonly seen traditional Chinese musical instruments, such as zither and *erhu*; 2. to know something about Chinese folk dance;	1) Does traditional music in China sound the same as that in your country? Are there any similarities between popular music in your country and that in China? 2) Are there any similarities between folk dances in your country and those in China?

Subjects	Learning Objectives	Sample Questions on Cross-cultural Communication
Music, Dance and Painting	3. to understand that China boasts a profound and unique tradition in painting; to get acquainted with some common Chinese landscape paintings.	3) What is the form of painting peculiar to your country?
Sports	1. to recognize shadowboxing as one of the most famous forms of *wushu* (martial arts) in China; to tell its differences from other forms of *wushu* (martial arts); 2. to get to know some popular sports in China, such as *pingpong*, badminton, swimming, and running.	1) Can you tell the differences between shadowboxing and the popular bodybuilding exercises in your country? 2) What are the popular sports in your country?
Transportation	1. to be familiar with the common means of transportation in China, i.e. bicycles, cars, buses, trolleybuses, subways, taxies, trains and planes; 2. to understand the role of bicycles as an important means of transportation in China; to learn something about the situation in which more and more people are owning cars in this country and be aware of the problems arising from this situation.	1) What are the common means of transportation in your country? 2) Of these, which is the most important? How does the bicycle stand in your transportation system?

Subjects	Learning Objectives	Sample Questions on Cross-cultural Communication
Mass Media	1. to gain some idea about radio broadcasting, television, newspapers, periodicals and other forms of mass media in China; 2. to name some of the powerful newspapers, periodicals, radio stations and TV stations in your country.	1) Can you name some influential TV stations, channels and radio stations in your country? 2) What is your favorite TV channel? Why?

Stage 3 Cultural Subjects and Learning Objectives

Subjects	Learning Objectives	Sample Questions on Cross-cultural Communication
Geography	1. to be familiar with the names of China's neighboring countries, including Russia, Korea, Vietnam, Japan, and India; 2. to understand their geographic relationships with China.	What are your neighboring countries? Can you name them in Chinese?
Architecture	To acquire a general knowledge of the names and basic features of traditional Chinese architecture, such as quadrangles, bungalows, etc.	Compare the residences and other buildings in your country and those in China.
Education	1. to gain some idea about the Chinese school system, which consists of kindergartens, primary schools, junior high schools, senior high schools, technical secondary schools, universities and adult education colleges;	1) Does your country have the same school system as China? 2) How many years does every stage of education take? 3) Are there any differences between the curricula in your country and those in China? If yes, what are they?

Subjects	Learning Objectives	Sample Questions on Cross-cultural Communication
Education	2. to understand and be familiar with the Chinese school curricula, i.e. compulsory and optional courses; and to know the names of major subjects and minor subjects.	
Customs and Etiquettes	1. to learn some knowledge about the Chinese way of giving and receiving presents. For instance, the Chinese people do not open presents in the face of their givers; 2. to gain some idea about the customs pertaining to birthday celebration. By tradition people eat noodles on their birthday as a symbol of longevity, but birthday cakes are gradually catching on nowadays; 3. to learn the basic Chinese terms when two persons bid goodbye: aside from *zaijian* 再见 (goodbye), the other commonly used terms upon leave-taking include *liubu* 留步 (don't bother to see me out) and *manzou* 慢走 (take care); to gain some idea about the etiquettes when people part ways. For instance, the host will most probably see someone off by escorting him or her for a distance.	1) How presents are given and taken in your country? 2) Do people in your country open presents right in front of their givers? 3) What are the customs pertaining to birthday celebration in your country? 4) Do people in your country use expressions like *manzou* 慢走 (take care) and *liubu* 留步 (don't bother to see me out) when seeing somebody off? Why?

Subjects	Learning Objectives	Sample Questions on Cross-cultural Communication
Music, Dance and Painting	1. to be acquainted with and appreciate some well-known classical and folk Chinese music; 2. to be acquainted with and appreciate some famous Chinese folk dances; 3. to get to know some prominent painters in Chinese history and their works.	1) Can you name some works of classical music, folk music and popular music in your country? 2) Are there any folk dances in your country? What are they? 3) Can you name some big-name painters in your country? What are their masterpieces? What do you think are their similarities to and differences from Chinese paintings?

Stage 4 Cultural Subjects and Learning Objectives

Subjects	Learning Objectives	Sample Questions on Cross-cultural Communication
Geography	1. to gain some basic idea about China's topographic features: China has complicated landforms with vast mountain areas; 2. to learn something about China's topographic features. For instance, the land descends gradually from west to east; 3. to know the names of famous mountains and rivers in China, such as the Yangtze River, the Yellow River, and Mount Tai.	1) Compare the topography of China with that of your country and your continent. List the topographic features of your country. 2) Do you know the topographic features of your country or your continent? Are they the same as China?

Appendix 3 Subjects and Learning Objectives on Chinese Culture

Subjects	Learning Objectives	Sample Questions on Cross-cultural Communication
Opera	1. to understand that China boasts a good variety of operas. Besides Peking Opera, known as the "national opera", there are Shaoxing Opera, Huangmei Opera and many other local operas; 2. to know some popular opera titles and their plots. For instance, *Romance of the West Chamber*.	1) Can you pinpoint some of the similarities between Chinese operas and yours? 2) Do your country's operas use make-ups that are similar to Chinese operas? 3) Are there any opera stories in your country that are similar to the Chinese opera *Lotus Lantern*?
Festivals	To gain some idea about the origins of the Spring Festival (Chinese Lunar New Year), Dragon Boat Festival and Mid-autumn Festival; to learn the legends about Nian the beast, Qu Yuan the poet, and Chang'er the Moon Goddess.	1) List some major festivals in your country and explain their origins. 2) Which festival do you think is as important to people in your country as the Spring Festival is to the Chinese people? Why?
Trans-portation	1. to understand bus stop signs in Chinese; 2. to understand the way trains are numbered in China. For instance, the letter Z is used in numbering for nonstop trains, the letter Y is used for tourist trains, the letter T is for express trains, and the letter K for fast trains.	1) How are bus stop signs in your country different from those in China? Which do you think is more user-friendly and why? 2) Can you explain the way flight numbers are indicated in your country? Can you give specific examples?

Subjects	Learning Objectives	Sample Questions on Cross-cultural Communication
Customs	1. to understand that the Spring Festival is the most important traditional festival in China; and to learn the customs pertaining to it, such as having New Year's Eve Dinner, pasting Spring Festival couplets on front doors, exchanging New Year courtesy visits, and eating dumplings; 2. to understand that the Dragon Boat Festival is another major Chinese festival; and to learn the customs pertaining to it, such as watching dragon boat races, eating *zongzi* (rice dumplings), and hanging mugworts up front doors; 3. to understand that the Mid-autumn Festival is a traditional occasion for family reunion; and to learn the customs pertaining to it, such as appreciating the moon while eating moon cakes.	1) During the Spring Festival, the Chinese people paste or hang the character *fu* 福 (meaning "good fortune") upside down, because in Chinese, this has the pleasant connotation of the forthcoming good fortune. Are there any similar practices in your country? 2) In your country, which festival is meant for family reunion? What are the customs?
Music, Dance and Painting	1. to acquire a deeper knowledge about Chinese music; and to learn some simple folk songs and popular ones; 2. to be acquainted with some common traditional music instruments and be able to identify their tones;	1) To say something about your understanding of Chinese music in light of your own country's music tradition. 2) Are there any dance forms popular both in China and in your country?

Subjects	Learning Objectives	Sample Questions on Cross-cultural Communication
Music, Dance and Painting	3. to know some popular dance forms in China; 4. to learn some artistic features of Chinese painting, such as *liu-bai* (meaning "blank spot", a traditional technique to leave some space untouched by the brush so that the objects in the picture do not appear too crowded), and the Great Freehand Style.	3) Tell us your understanding of Chinese painting in light of the artistic features of paintings in your country.
Sports	1. to gain some idea about where your country and China stand in every athletic sport in the world sports arena; 2. to know something about Liu Xiang, Yao Ming and other athletes of world fame.	1) Which sport events in your country have reached a high level in the international sports arena? 2) Name some world-level sports stars in your country.
Mass Media	1. to be aware of the characteristics of China's websites, such as .cn; 2. to try to log in them to look for needed information.	List some suffixes frequently found in your country's websites, such as .edu and .com.

Stage 5 Cultural Subjects and Learning Objectives

Subjects	Learning Objectives	Sample Questions on Cross-cultural Communication
Climate and Geography	1. to understand that China has varied climates, which are characterized by cold and dry winter and hot and wet summer;	1) Compare the climate in your country and that in China. 2) Tell the differences between your country and China in administrative division.

Subjects	Learning Objectives	Sample Questions on Cross-cultural Communication
Climate and Geography	2. to know something about the administrative division in China: there are 34 administrative units at provincial level, with prefectures and counties under their jurisdiction; 3. to be acquainted with some municipalities directly under the central government such as Beijing, Shanghai, Tianjin and Chongqing and provincial capital cities such as Guangzhou in Guangdong province; 4. to know the names of major cities in China and their geographic positions.	3) Are there any cities in your country that have fostered sister relationships with cities in China? Can you name some of the sister cities?
History	1. to acquire some general knowledge about major periods, ages and dynasties in Chinese history, such as the Spring and Autumn period, the Qin dynasty, the Han dynasty, the Tang dynasty, the Ming dynasty and the Qing dynasty; 2. to be acquainted with major events in Chinese history, such as the Opium War (1840-1842) and the foundation of the People's Republic of China in 1949;	1) Compare the Chinese history with the history of your country. Can you tell which historical period in your country is synchronous to a major Chinese period? 2) How much do you know about the history of the relationship between your country and China?

Subjects	Learning Objectives	Sample Questions on Cross-cultural Communication
History	3. to get to know some eminent figures in Chinese history, such as Qinshihuang, Emperor Taizong of the Tang dynasty, Qu Yuan, Confucius, Sima Qian, and Mao Zedong.	
Contemporary China	1. to gain some idea about the general financial situation of contemporary China, including the names of major banks, stocks, funds and foreign banks; 2. to understand the basic characteristics of economic development in China; 3. to understand the basic conditions of rural China: there remains a wide gap in economic development between south and north and between east and west; it is a common phenomenon in China for farmers to quit agriculture and become migrant workers in cities; 4. to acquire some general knowledge about regional differences and the difference between urban and rural areas in China: east China outgrows west China; villages trail behind cities in economic development; there is a yawning gap between urban and rural areas; industrialization has brought about environmental pollution problems.	1) Check out if any financial institutions in your country have invested in China, and find out why such investments are made. 2) Compare the basic characteristics of economic development in your country and those in China. 3) Analyze the differences between the rural areas in your country and those in China. 4) Is there any development gap between the urban and rural areas in your country?

Subjects	Learning Objectives	Sample Questions on Cross-cultural Communication
Literature and Opera	1. to know the names of the four major Chinese classical novels and learn their plots; 2. to get to know some renowned contemporary writers and learn the plots of some of their masterpieces; 3. to acquire some general knowledge about the history and evolvement of Peking Opera.	1) Name some writers in your country who lived in the same period as the prominent Chinese writers you've studied, and list their representative works. 2) What are the differences between operas in your country and Peking Opera?
Travel	To know the names of some well-known tourist attractions and scenic spots, such as the landscape of Guilin, the army of terracotta warriors and horses in Xi'an, the Forbidden City and the Great Wall in Beijing.	Can you name some tourist attractions in China that are similar to those in your country? In what ways are they similar to each other?
Customs	1. to know something about the folkways in some famous tourist destinations, such as the folk songs, dances and other cultural forms of the ethnic groups in Yunnan; 2. to understand the time-honored tradition of "respecting the aged and loving the young" cherished by the Chinese people;	1) Conduct a survey on some fellow citizens of Chinese descedant about their different customs and folkways from yours. 2) What are the differences between your country and China in people's attitudes towards senior citizens? Give your understanding of and comment on the ageing problem confronting the world population.

Appendix 3　Subjects and Learning Objectives on Chinese Culture

Subjects	Learning Objectives	Sample Questions on Cross-cultural Communication
Customs	3. to know something about the outdated Chinese tradition of women being inferior to men, and the ongoing effort to advocate equality between men and women; 4. to gain some idea about the "Golden Weeks" (week-long holidays) in China and their social repercussions. For instance, the week-long National Day holiday, and the huge flow of tourists and shopping fever occurring during the "Golden Weeks".	3) Does sex discrimination exist in your country? What's your view on inequality between men and women in real life? 4) Do you have holidays like the Golden Weeks in China? If any, what do your people mainly do during such holidays?
Food	1. to learn something about Chinese cooking: common methods of cooking include frying, stir-frying, boiling, deep-frying and roasting; 2. to acquire some knowledge about the dietary habits of the Chinese people. For instance, southerners tend to have a sweet tooth, while northerners prefer salty dishes; the staple food is rice in the south or wheat flour in the north; the Chinese are in the habit of sharing dishes during mealtime.	1) Tell the differences between the Chinese way of cooking and yours. 2) What's your view on Chinese people sharing dishes during mealtime? List its advantages and disadvantages in light of the dietary habit in your country.

Subjects	Learning Objectives	Sample Questions on Cross-cultural Communication
Specialties	1. to understand and learn the names and basic properties of traditional Chinese medicines: some are cold in nature while some others hot; and to remember the names of some common herbal medicines, such as mint; 2. to be acquainted with some well-known teas, such as *Longjing* tea and *Tieguanyin*; and to know their places of origin; 3. to be familiar with some brand-name drinks, such as *Maotai* (liquor) and Qingdao Beer.	1) How do you compare the traditional Chinese medicine and Western medicine? 2) What are the differences between China and your own country in wine-associated culture?

Appendix 4 Sample Activities for Chinese Language Teaching

Stage 1 for School Students

Subject		Greetings	
Activity Plans	Preparation	Prepare pictures of people in different colors, styles and sizes, and cards with captions in Chinese characters: family members, friends, and greetings.	
	Subject-oriented Activities	1. greeting	Greet different people (students' performance).
		2. sing greeting songs	1) learn to sing greeting songs; 2) write out the lyrics in Chinese characters or *Pinyin*.
	Progress Assessment	Listening—students can listen and recognize different greetings with teacher guidance; Speaking—students can say simple greetings with teacher guidance; Reading—students can read basic Chinese characters and *Pinyin* with teacher guidance; Writing—students can write the Chinese characters and *Pinyin* they have learned with teacher guidance.	

Stage 1 for Non-School Learners

Subject	Greetings		
Activity Plans	Preparation	1. prepare pictures of well-known public figures in different colors, styles and sizes, with captions of their names and titles (in Chinese characters and *Pinyin*); 2. prepare chest placards with the appellations or titles of family numbers, colleagues and friends in Chinese characters; 3. choose the right words, put (or write) them around the pictures; 4. hang on the blackboard a poster with various greetings on it.	
	Subject-oriented Activities	1. greeting	Role-play going to a party and greeting different public figures (performed by students holding pictures of those figures).
		2. visiting	1) role-play visiting your friend's house and greeting his/her family members (performed by students, each with a chest placard). e.g. "王先生，您好！""李小姐，你好！" 2) role-play visiting a company and greeting people there. e.g. "你好，李小姐。""再见，李先生。"
	Progress Assessment	Listening—students can recognize different greetings； Speaking—students can say simple greetings； Reading—students can read out basic Chinese characters that have been learned； Writeing—students can write the Chinese characters used in greetings.	

Stage 2 for School Students

Subject		My Dog	
Activity Plans	Preparation	Prepare pictures of dogs in different colors and sizes, as well as cards with colours and adjectives in Chinese characters.	
	Subject-oriented Activities	1. distinguishing dogs	With teacher guidance, students should: 1) describe dogs of different colors; 2) describe dogs of different sizes; 3) make a simple description of dogs.
		2. coloring the pictures of dogs	Apply colors to pictures of dogs.
	Progress Assessment	Listening—students can recognize different adjectives; Speaking—students can describe the sizes and colors of different dogs; Reading—students can read out the basic Chinese characters required to master; Writeing—students can write the Chinese characters that have been learned.	

87

Stage 2 for Non-School Learners

Subject		Timetable	
Activity Plans	Preparation	1. prepare a clock; 2. prepare cards with clocks showing different time; 3. prepare cards with names of various activities and places; 4. prepare a brief timetable and hang it on the wall.	
	Subject-oriented Activities	1. identifying time	With teacher guidance, students learn to: 1) tell time; 2) identify different time.

Subject	Timetable		
Activity Plans	Subject-oriented Activities	2. a pleasant morning	1) do Q&A about time; 2) the teacher uses different cards to ask students questions about the time they get up, have breakfast, go to work and so on.
		3. a daily schedule	With teacher guidance, students learn to: 1) tell different time; 2) describe the arrangements of a day according to the schedule.
	Progress Assessment	Listening—with teacher guidance, students can listen and recognize words about time and activities; Speaking—students can speak with correct pronunciation and rignt tones and can make brief descriptions; Reading—students can read out words of activities required to master; Writing—students can write words of activities required to master.	

Stage 3 for School Students

Subject	Shopping		
Activity Plans	Preparation	Collect names and prices of some commodities, and prepare cards, pictures with the names of commodities and RMB prices on them, as well as real commodities.	
	Subject-oriented Activities	1. buying	1) make clear the commodities you want to buy. e.g. "我要这个。" "我买牛奶。" 2) ask for names and prices of commodities. e.g. "这是什么？" "多少钱？" 3) make clear whether you will take it or not. e.g. "要一个。" "不要了，谢谢。"

Subject			Shopping	
Activity Plans	Subject-oriented Activities	2. selling	1) greet customers. e.g. "你好！" 2) ask what customers want to buy. e.g. "您买什么？" 3) introduce the commodities (names, prices and so on). e.g. "这是毛笔。" "五块钱。" Say some commonly used sentences about changes. e.g. "一共多少钱？" "给你 20 块。" 4) say thanks. e.g. "给您，谢谢。" 5) bid farewell. e.g. "再见！"	
	Progress Assessment	1. Students can check among themselves: Who has bought the largest amount of commodities today? What has he/she bought? At what price? 2. Each student should make a shopping list and write down the commodities they need and the prices.		

Stage 3 for Non-School Learners

Subject			Dining	
Activity Plans	Preparation	1. prepare pictures of dishes, beverage and staple food; 2. prepare a menu with names and prices of dishes and beverage; 3. prepare cards marked with RMB prices.		
	Subject-oriented Activities	1. at the canteen	Role-play customers dining at the canteen: 1) greet people. e.g. "你好！" 2) make clear the food you want to order. e.g. "您要什么？" "要这个。" 3) enquire. e.g. "要咖啡吗？"	
		2. at a restaurant	Role-play customers dining at a restaurant, while the rest of the class put down the names of the dishes you have ordered: 1) greet guests. e.g. "欢迎。" "请坐。" "你们几位？" 2) order dishes. e.g. "一份沙拉。" "两瓶果汁。" 3) pay the bill. e.g. "一共 20 块。" 4) bid farewell. e.g. "再见！"	

Subject		Dining
Activity Plans	Progress Assessment	1. Students can tell the names and prices of the dishes sold today; 2. Students can tell the names and prices of some dishes; 3. Students can read simple menus and understand prices listed on the menu; 4. Students can write down the prices of commodities.

Stage 4 for School Students

Subject		Shopping	
Activity Plans	Preparation	1. find out the prices of some commodities in different shops; 2. prepare pictures of some commodities and some real commodities; 3. put up a small counter.	
	Subject-oriented Activities	1. buying	1) ask to look at some commodities. e.g. "请拿一下儿那个。""给我看看那件毛衣。" 2) ask for the prices, colors, and sizes of different commodities. e.g. "这个多少钱？""有白色的吗？""有小号的吗？" 3) make brief comments on the commodities. e.g. "有点儿贵。""大了点儿。" 4) decide whether to buy or not. e.g. "要一件。""不要了，谢谢。"
		2. selling	1) greet customers. e.g. "你好！""欢迎光临！" 2) ask what customers want to buy.
	Progress Assessment	Students can take the commodities they've bought back home and ask for comments from their family members.	

Stage 4 for Non-School Learners

Subject		Shopping	
Activity Plans	Preparation	1. find out the prices of some clothes in different shops; 2. prepare some pictures or clothes; 3. put up a small counter.	
	Subject-oriented Activities	1.buying clothes	1) ask to look at some clothes carefully. e.g. "请拿一下儿那个。""给我看看那件毛衣。" 2) ask for the prices, colors, and sizes of the clothes. e.g. "这个多少钱？""有白色的吗？""有小号的吗？" 3) make brief comments on the clothes. e.g. "有点儿贵。""大了点儿。" 4) decide whether to buy or not. e.g. "要一件。""不要了，谢谢。"
		2. selling clothes	1) greet customers. e.g. "你好！""欢迎光临！""想买点什么？" 2) ask what customers want to buy.
	Progress Assessment	1. Students can put on the new clothes and ask friends to make comments on them; 2. Students can write a list of quoted prices.	

Stage 5 for School Students

Subject		Register for an Activity
Activity Plans	Preparation	1. find the ads of a travel agency (training course or club) you are interested in; 2. prepare a tourist map; 3. prepare a registration form; 4. prepare your ID card and driver's license.

91

Subject			Register for an Activity
Activity Plans	Subject-oriented Activities	1. discussion	1) put forth your intention. e.g. "我想假期报个团去中国旅游。" 2) express your attitude (approval, hesitation or disapproval), and give your reason. e.g. "太好了，我也正想去中国看看呢。听说随团旅游很便宜。" 3) discuss or argue. e.g. "这个季节南京太热了，不如去东北。""选哪家旅行社比较好？"
		2. registration procedure	1) fill the registration form. e.g. "请您用钢笔填写。""请填上详细的通讯地址。" 2) go through the formalities (have photos taken, sign your name, get the form sealed, and pay the fee). e.g. "请您在这里签一下儿名。""等签证下来我们会通知您。" 3) sign the contract. e.g. "请您再仔细看一遍合同，有没有异议？""旅游保险包括进去了吗？"
	Progress Assessment		1. Students can make a detailed travel plan; 2. Students can understand FAQ at the Customs; 3. Students can understand and answer simple questions; 4. Students can read and understand tourist information; 5. Students can fill in simple forms.

Stage 5 for Non-School Learners

Subject		Joining a Club
Activity Plans	Preparation	1. prepare ads of some clubs; 2. prepare pictures of club activities; 3. prepare an registration form.

Subject			Joining a Club
Activity Plans	Subject-oriented Activities	1. discussion	1) state your purpose. e.g. "我想加入篮球俱乐部。" 2) express your attitude (approval, hesitation or disapproval). e.g. "太好了，我也正想报名呢。" 3) discuss or argue. e.g. "你不如加入我们合唱团。"
		2. registration procedure	1) enquire. e.g. "请问，每周活动几次？" 2) give positive information. e.g. "我们在上次联赛中获得了第二名。" 3) fill the registration form. e.g. "请填上您的联系方式。" 4) go through the formalities (pay the fee and sign the contract). e.g. "请您在这里签一下儿名。"
		3. welcoming ceremony	1) hold welcome ceremony for new members, introducing members of the club; 2) get known to each other.
		4. competition	1) watch a competition on video; 2) organize a competition within a class.
	Progress Assessment		1. Students can write an introduction of a club； 2. Students can understand what people say when introducing each other in certain situations； 3. Students can explain why they choose to join the club； 4. Students can write a report on a sports competition.

Appendix 5 Grammatical Items

Stage 1 Grammatical Items

Objectives	Know and master: 1. basic word order 2. common sentence patterns 3. general questions 4. numerals and measure words 5. personal pronouns 6. demonstrative pronouns 7. common adverbs of degree 8. basic expressions to describe a person or an object 9. negative sentences with 不		
Content	**Grammar Items**	**Structure**	**Examples**
	1. subject-predicate sentences	主语＋动词＋宾语	我姓王。
	1.1 是 sentences	主语＋是＋宾语	玛丽是美国人。
	1.2 有 sentences	主语＋有＋宾语	我有一个弟弟。
		主语＋没有＋宾语	我没有电子词典。
	2. general questions with 吗 吧 呢	小句＋吗?	玛丽是大学生吗?
		小句＋吧?	约翰是美国人吧?
		小句，名词／代词＋呢?	我是中国人，你呢?

Grammar Items	Structure	Examples
3. sentences with an adjective predicate	主语＋副词＋形容词	我很高兴。 玛丽非常漂亮。
4. sentences with a noun predicate	主语＋年龄／籍贯等	玛丽 20 岁。 王明上海人。
5. negative sentences with 不	主语＋不＋动词短语	我不喜欢唱歌。
6. imperative sentences: for polite request	请＋动词！	请进！请坐！
7. exclamatory sentences	真＋形容词！ 太＋形容词＋了！	真好！ 太棒了！
8. personal pronouns	你、我、他、她、您	您贵姓？
8.1 plural form of personal pronouns	你们、我们、他们	我们学习汉语。
8.2 demonstrative pronouns	这、那	这位是布朗先生。 那个人是美国人。
9. adverbs of degree as adverbial	很、非常、真、太	布朗非常忙。
10. numerals	1~100	我爸爸 66 岁。
11. measure words	个、名	我家有两个男孩。 我们班有 25 名学生。
12. conjunctions	A 和 B	我和弟弟 爸爸、妈妈和我

Content

Stage 2 Grammatical Items

Objectives	Know and master: 1. basic expressions of time, place, and location 2. RMB, sum of money 3. structures and functions of adverbials and attributives 4. special questions 5. existential sentences 6. expressions of wishes		
Content	**Grammar Items**	**Structure**	**Examples**
	1. expressions of time		
	1.1 indication of 年 月 日	___年___月___日	2007 年 12 月 5 日
	1.2 indication of 星期	星期___	星期一～星期天
	1.3 indication of a certain point of time	___点___分 差___分___点	8 点、8 点 10 分 差 5 分 8 点 差 1 刻 10 点
	2. expressions of the sum of money in RMB	___元／块___角／毛___分	105 块 6 角 8 分
	3. sentences with a noun predicate	主语＋时间 主语＋钱数	今天 12 月 6 号。 明天星期四。 现在 9 点 20。 这本书 32 块 5 毛。 3 斤苹果 10 块钱。
	4. adverbials of time	主语＋时间状语＋动词短语	我每天早上 6 点半起床。

96

	Grammar Items	Structure	Examples
Content	5. adverbials of place	主语＋在＋地点／处所＋动词短语	我在一家电脑公司工作。
	6. possessive	名词／代词＋（的）＋名词	这是我的书。 她是我弟弟。
	7. directional words		
	7.1 simple directional words	上、下、左、右、前、后、东、西、南、北、中	
	7.2 compound directional words	简单方位词＋面／边	上面、上边、东面、东边、西面、西边
	7.3 directional phrases	处所名词＋简单方位词＋（面／边）	桌子上、窗外、银行前边、学校西边
	8. special questions	什么、谁、哪、哪儿、几、多少、多大、什么时候	你叫什么名字？ 他是谁？ 你是哪国人？ 你在哪儿上学？ 现在几点了？ 你的孩子多大了？ 这本书多少钱？ 你什么时候开学？
	9. existential sentences		
	9.1 在 sentences	方位词（词组）＋在＋方位词组	北京大学在清华大学西边。

Grammar Items	Structure	Examples
9.2 有 sentences	方位词组＋有＋名词（词组）	桌子上有两本书。
9.3 是 sentences	方位词组＋是＋名词（词组）	图书馆西边是运动场。
10. expresssions of distance	A点＋离＋B点＋远／近／距离数	北京大学离清华大学很近。
11. expressions of wishes with 要　想	主语＋要＋名词	我要一瓶可乐。
	主语＋要／想＋动词短语	我想去中国。 玛丽要去图书馆。
12. 的 sentences	名词／代词＋的	这是玛丽的。
	形容词＋的	红的好看。
13. reduplication of a verb & verb with 一下儿	动词重叠	我试试这件衣服。
	动词＋一下儿	你看一下儿这本书。
14. common measure words	件、条、块、张、斤	一件衬衣、两条裤子、三块面包、四张桌子、五斤苹果
15. adverbs of scope		
15.1 都	都＋动词短语	我们都学习汉语。
15.2 也	也＋动词短语	他也是美国人。

Content

98

Stage 3 Grammatical Items

Objectives	1. common prepositions 2. basic comparative structures 3. progressive aspect 4. particle 了 5. negative sentences with 没（有） 6. common modal verbs		
Content	**Grammar Items**	**Structure**	**Examples**
	1. prepositions: preceding words of place, or direction		
	1.1 从	从＋起点＋动词短语	我刚从英国回来。
	1.2 向	向＋方向＋动词短语	（你）一直向北走。
	1.3 往	往＋方向＋动词短语	往右拐。
	1.4 从……到……	从＋起点＋到＋终点	从这儿到你们大学怎么走？
	2. progressive aspect	主语＋正＋动词短语＋呢	布朗正看书呢。
		主语＋在＋动词短语＋（呢）	玛丽在睡觉（呢）。
		主语＋正在＋动词短语＋（呢）	王先生正在打电话（呢）。
	3. particle 着	主语＋动词＋着＋名词	布朗戴着一副眼镜。
	4. existential sentences	方位词组＋动词＋着＋名词（词组）	墙上挂着一张世界地图。

99

Grammar Items	Structure	Examples
5. particle 了	数量词／名词＋了	我儿子 8 岁了。 秋天了。
	主语＋形容词／动词＋了	花红了。 玛丽病了。
	小句＋了	我昨天去王府井了。
	主语＋动词＋了＋数量／动量＋（名）	我买了两件衬衫。 这本书我看了两遍。
6. negative sentences with 没（有）	主语＋没（有）＋动词短语	我没有看电视。
7. expressions meaning "(not) as…as"	……跟／和……（不）一样	我跟你不一样。
	……跟／和……（不）一样＋形容词	他和我一样高。
8. comparative structures		
8.1 comparative structures	A＋比＋B＋形容词	今天比昨天冷。
8.2 negative comparative structures	A＋没有＋B＋形容词	你没有玛丽高。
9. adverbs 最	最＋形容词／动词短语	这是中国最大的城市。

Content

100

Grammar Items	Structure	Examples
10. sentences with double objects	主语＋直接宾语＋间接宾语	玛丽给我一本书。 找你两块钱。
11. converbal structures	主语＋动词短语1+动词短语2	我坐地铁去上班。 我用筷子吃饭。
12. alternative questions	……还是……?	你喝茶还是喝咖啡? 你去还是我去?
13. affirmative-negative questions	主语＋Adj. 不 Adj. ?	那件衣服贵不贵?
	主语 +V 不 V+（宾语）?	你来不来?
	主语 +V 没 V+（宾语）?	你看没看电影?
14. questions with 怎么	主语＋怎么＋动词短语?	这个字怎么念? 去银行怎么走?
15. questions with 怎么样? 好吗? 可以吗? 行吗?	名词词组＋怎么样?	这本汉语书怎么样?
	小句，怎么样?	我们坐公共汽车去，怎么样?
	小句，好吗?	我们吃中餐，好吗?
	小句，可以吗?	我这样说，可以吗?
	小句，行吗?	这样写，行吗?
16. modal verbs		
16.1 能	能＋动词短语	玛丽能来。

	Grammar Items	Structure	Examples
Content	16.2 会	会＋动词短语	我会打网球。
	16.3 可以	可以＋动词短语	这儿可以拍照。
	16.4 应该	应该＋动词短语	你应该早点儿来。
	16.5 愿意	愿意＋动词短语	我愿意学习汉语。
	17. prepositons 跟 and 给		
	17.1 跟	跟＋某人（一起）＋动词短语	我跟他一起去。
	17.2 给	给＋某人＋动词短语	我给爸爸打电话

Stage 4 Grammatical Items

Objectives	Know and master: 1. common adverbs of time 2. particle 过 3. complement of time 4. complement of action 5. the pattern of 是……的 6. pivotal sentences 7. common compound sentences

	Grammar Items	Structure	Examples
Content	1. adverbs of time used as adverbial:		
	1.1 还	还＋动词短语	玛丽还在看电视。 他们还没下班呢。

	Grammar Items	Structure	Examples
Content	1.2 已经	已经＋动词短语	他们已经下班了。
	1.3 再 and 又	主语＋再＋动词短语	你再听一遍。
		主语＋又＋动词短语	他又说了一遍。
	1.4 就 and 才	主语＋（时间）＋就＋动词短语	我就来。 我今天6点就起床了。
		主语＋（时间）＋才＋动词短语	他才来。 他今天8点半才来上班。
	2. particle 了	该＋名词短语／动词短语＋了	该你了。 该上课了。
		（就／快）要＋动词短语＋了	快要下雨了。 飞机就要起飞了。
		能愿动词＋动词短语＋了	我能走了。 我会说汉语了。 你可以下班了。
		不＋动词短语＋了	我不去了。 他不喝酒了。
		主语＋动词＋了＋名词＋就／再＋动词短语	我吃了饭再去。 我下了课就来你这儿了。
	3. particle 过	主语＋（没）＋动词＋过＋名词（短语）	我去过中国。 我没看过这部电影。
	4. complement of time	动词＋时量	我吃过两次烤鸭。

Grammar Items	Structure	Examples
	动词短语＋时量＋了	我来北京三年了。 他大学毕业 10 年了。
	动词＋了＋时量＋（名词）	我打了两个小时网球。
	动词＋了＋时量＋（名词）＋了	我打了两个小时网球了。
5. complement of action		
5.1 次	动词＋数＋次	我去过三次上海。
5.2 遍	动词＋数＋遍	这本书我看过三遍。
5.3 趟	动词＋数＋趟	我去了一趟香港。
6. comparative structures	A＋比＋B＋更／还＋形容词	今天比昨天还冷。
	A＋比＋B＋形容词＋数量	我比我弟弟大三岁。
	A＋比＋B＋形容词＋一点儿／多了	他的汉语比我好多了。
7. pivotal sentences	主语＋请／让／叫／＋某人＋动词短语	我请王老师看电影。 妈妈不让我抽烟。
8. the pattern of 是……的		
8.1 to emphasize time	主语＋是＋时间＋动词短语＋的	我是 1968 年出生的。

Appendix 5　Grammatical Items

	Grammar Items	Structure	Examples
Content	8.2 to emphasize location	主语＋是＋空间方位＋动词短语＋的	我是在北京出生的。 他是从美国来的。
	8.3 to emphasize means of action	主语＋是＋方式＋动词短语＋的	他是坐飞机来的。
	9. questions with 怎么了	名词＋怎么了？	你怎么了？
	10. compound sentences	先……，再……	你先写作业，一会儿再看电视。
		因为……，所以……	因为很忙，所以我没去。
		如果（要是）……，就……	要是下雨，我们就不去了。
		不但……，而且……	他不但学习汉语，而且还学习西班牙语。
		虽然……，但是……	虽然很累，但是我一定要完成作业。

Stage 5 Grammatical Items

Objectives	Know and master: 1. complements of result, of direction, of possibility and of degree 2. 把 sentences 3. passive voice 4. compound sentences

	Grammar Items	Structure	Examples
Content	1. complement of result		
	1.1 with adjectives	动词＋形容词	衣服洗干净了。
	1.2 with 完	动词＋完	作业写完了。
	1.3 with 到	动词＋到	飞机票买到了。
	1.4 with 好	动词＋好	晚饭做好了。
	1.5 negative form of complement of result	没＋动词＋结果补语	晚饭还没做好。
	2. turning complement of result into complement of possibility	动词＋得＋补语	
	2.1 positive form	动词＋得＋补语　或 能＋动词＋补语	这么多作业，你写得完吗？ 我能买到去上海的飞机票。
	2.2 negative form	动词＋不＋补语	这么多作业,我写不完。
	3. commonly used complement of possibility	看得见／看不见 睡得着／睡不着	飞机看不见了。 我睡不着。
	4. complement of direction	动词＋得／不＋了	明天的课我上不了。

Appendix 5　Grammatical Items

	Grammar Items	Structure	Examples
Content	4.1 simple complement of direction	动词＋来／去	上来、上去、下来、下去、进来、进去、出来、出去、过来、过去、回来、回去、起来
	4.2 combined complement of direction	动词＋上／下＋来／去	拿上来、搬下去
		动词＋进／出＋来／去	跑进来、走出去
		动词＋回＋来／去	走回来、寄回去
		动词＋过＋来／去	跳过来、跳过去
		动词＋起＋来	站起来
	4.3 extensional uses of complement of direction	动词＋上	关上窗户
		动词＋下	脱下大衣
		动词＋起来	笑起来、做起来
		动词＋下去	说下去
	4.4 turning complement of direction into complement of possibility	动词＋得／不＋趋向补语	进得来、进不来 拿得起来、拿不起来
	5. complement of degree	动词＋得＋程度副词＋形容词	玛丽跑得很快。 我今天吃得不太多。

	Grammar Items	Structure	Examples
Content	5.1 complement of degree	施事＋动词＋受事＋动词＋得＋形容词	玛丽说汉语说得很好。
	5.2 the position of the recipient of the verb in complement of degree	施事＋受事＋动词＋得＋形容词	玛丽篮球打得不太好。
		受事＋施事＋动词＋得＋形容词	这首歌玛丽唱得很好听。
	6. 把 sentences	主语＋把＋名词＋动词＋补充成分	
		主语＋把＋名词＋动词＋形容词	我把房间打扫干净了。
		主语＋把＋名词＋动词＋趋向	你把铅笔递过来。
		主语＋把＋名词＋动词＋在＋地方	我把车停在学校门口了。
		主语＋把＋名词＋动词＋到＋地方	请你把我的包拿到205房间。
		主语＋把＋名词＋动词＋给＋某人	他把这封信交给了玛丽。
	7. passive voice		
	7.1 notional passive	受事＋动词＋补充成分	作业写完了。 这顿饭吃得很香。
	7.2 passive with 被	受事＋被（＋施事）＋动词＋补充成分	我的腿被守门员撞伤了。

108

Appendix 5　Grammatical Items

	Grammar Items	Structure	Examples
Content	8. compound sentences	受事＋是＋施事＋动词＋的	这本书是马老师编的。
		既然……就……	既然这么贵，我就不买了。
		即使……也……	即使再贵点儿，我也要买。
		无论……都……	无论多远，我都要去。
		不是……就是……	周末他不是睡懒觉就是出去玩。
		宁可……也……	我宁可饿死，也不吃这种菜。

国际汉语教学通用课程大纲

International Curriculum
for Chinese Language Education

国家汉语国际推广领导小组办公室
The Office of Chinese Language Council International

外语教学与研究出版社
FOREIGN LANGUAGE TEACHING AND RESEARCH PRESS
北京　BEIJING

图书在版编目(CIP)数据

国际汉语教学通用课程大纲 = International Curriculum for Chinese Language Education：英汉对照／国家汉语国际推广领导小组办公室编 . — 北京：外语教学与研究出版社，2008.3
ISBN 978 - 7 - 5600 - 7401 - 6

Ⅰ . 国… Ⅱ . 国… Ⅲ . 对外汉语教学—教学大纲 Ⅳ . H195.2

中国版本图书馆 CIP 数据核字 (2008) 第 037862 号

出　版　人：于春迟
责任编辑：潘瑞芳
封面设计：张　峰
版式设计：平　原
出版发行：外语教学与研究出版社
社　　　址：北京市西三环北路 19 号 (100089)
网　　　址：http://www.fltrp.com
印　　　刷：中国农业出版社印刷厂
开　　　本：787×1092　1/16
印　　　张：17　插页 1 张
版　　　次：2008 年 3 月第 1 版　2010 年 3 月第 5 次印刷
书　　　号：ISBN 978 - 7 - 5600 - 7401 - 6
定　　　价：49.00 元
＊　　　＊　　　＊
如有印刷、装订质量问题，请与出版社联系
联系电话：(010)61207896　　电子邮箱：zhijian@fltrp.com
制售盗版必究　举报查实奖励
版权保护办公室举报电话：(010)88817519
物料号：174010001

编 委 会

主任：许　琳

委员（以姓氏笔画为序）：

马箭飞、王永利、白建华（美国）、刘　骏（美国）、
吴坚立（澳大利亚）、赵国成、赵金铭、赵　勇（美国）、
徐　弘（加拿大）、龚亚夫、谢绵绵（加拿大）

研 制 组

组长：赵金铭、徐　弘（加拿大）、许　琳、
　　　马箭飞、赵国成、王永利

主要参与人员（以姓氏笔画为序）：

丁安琪	（北京外国语大学）
马德安	（美国麻州国宾中学）
方欣欣	（加拿大阿尔伯塔省教育厅）
毛　悦	（北京语言大学）
王　波	（北京外国语大学）
王蕊文	（美国西点军校）
王锦红	（国家汉办/孔子学院总部）
王　巍	（吉林大学）
邓秀均	（中央民族大学）
冯　睿	（加拿大阿尔伯塔大学）
古川裕	（日本大阪外国语大学）
白乐桑	（法国国家东方语言文化学院）
白建华	（美国肯杨大学）
刘长征	（北京语言大学）

刘芳芳	（北京外国语大学）
刘 骏	（美国亚利桑那大学）
吕滇雯	（北京外国语大学）
孙文正	（国家汉办 / 孔子学院总部）
朱 俐	（美国 CET 学术项目）
朱 勇	（北京外国语大学）
毕杰夫	（美国"海外学年"项目）
吴坚立	（澳大利亚中文教师联会）
吴勇毅	（华东师范大学）
吴思娜	（北京外国语大学）
宋连谊	（英国伦敦大学）
张 红	（北京外国语大学）
张向华	（北京芳草地小学）
张 彤	（美国"海外学年"项目）
张彤辉	（国家汉办 / 孔子学院总部）
张学增	（德国纽伦堡爱尔兰根孔子学院）
张桂元	（哥伦比亚中国文化基金会）
张曼荪	（美国威廉大学）
张 锦	（美国麻省理工学院）
李 焱	（美国"海外学年"项目）
李 燕	（北京语言大学）
来静青	（北京外国语大学）
杨少芳	（北京外国语大学）
杨丽珍	（美国明尼苏达大学）
杨 慧	（北京外国语大学）
陈小明	（北京外国语大学）

陈山木　　　　　　　　（加拿大中文教学学会）

陈　昕　　　　　　　　（北京芳草地小学）

麦文贤　　　　　　　　（美国爱荷华大学）

卓素珊　　　　　　　　（澳大利亚维州中文教师协会）

孟柱亿　　　　　　　　（韩国外国语大学）

岳　薇　　　　　　　　（北京外国语大学）

林秀琴　　　　　　　　（首都师范大学）

林游岚　　　　　　　　（全美中小学中文教师协会）

武　娟　　　　　　　　（北京外国语大学）

郑梅英　　　　　　　　（北京市五十五中学）

姚道中　　　　　　　　（美国夏威夷大学）

施仲谋　　　　　　　　（香港大学）

柯彼德　　　　　　　　（德国美因兹大学）

贺大卫　　　　　　　　（澳大利亚墨尔本大学）

贺　军　　　　　　　　（北京外国语大学）

赵　菁　　　　　　　　（北京语言大学）

赵金铭　　　　　　　　（北京语言大学）

赵　勇　　　　　　　　（美国密西根州立大学）

赵雪梅　　　　　　　　（北京语言大学）

徐　弘　　　　　　　　（加拿大爱德蒙顿教育局）

桑迪·福斯特　　　　　（加拿大爱德蒙顿教育局）

钱苏平　　　　　　　　（澳大利亚翩丽艾森顿文法学校）

顾百里　　　　　　　　（美国威廉大学）

崔永华　　　　　　　　（北京语言大学）

崔颂仁　　　　　　　　（美国博敦大学）

梁冬梅　　　　　　　　（北京外国语大学）

梁彦民　　　　　　（北京语言大学）

龚亚夫　　　　　　（人民教育出版社）

曾妙芬　　　　　　（美国弗吉尼亚大学）

谢绵绵　　　　　　（加拿大爱德蒙顿教育局）

韩　曦　　　　　　（新西兰外语联合会）

谭春健　　　　　　（北京语言大学）

魏红霞　　　　　　（澳大利亚维多利亚州教育及幼儿发展部）

魏崇新　　　　　　（北京外国语大学）

说　明

1. 目　的

为顺应世界各地汉语教学迅速发展的趋势，满足各国对汉语教学内容规范化的需求，国家汉办／孔子学院总部组织研制了《国际汉语教学通用课程大纲》（以下简称《大纲》）。

《大纲》是对汉语作为第二语言课程目标与内容的梳理和描述，旨在为汉语教学机构和教师在教学计划制订、学习者语言能力评测和教材编写等方面提供参考依据和参照标准。

2. 原　则

2.1　科学性原则

《大纲》以语言交际能力理论为指导，参考和借鉴了多种外语和第二语言教学大纲的经验和成果，吸收了国际汉语教学的经验，并在较大范围内进行了调研。在制订方法上力求既凭借经验，又注重实证，理论与实际相结合，具有较强的科学性、典型性。

2.2　实用性原则

《大纲》从指导国际汉语教学实践的角度出发，对课程目标及学习者所应具备的语言知识、语言技能、策略和文化意识等方面，进行了分级分类描述。同时，还提供了《汉语教学话题及内容建议表》、《汉语教学话题及内容举例表》、《中国文化题材及文化任务举例表》、《汉语教学任务活动示范列表》、《常用汉语语法项目分级表》、《汉语拼音声母、韵母与声调》、《常用汉语 800 字表》、《常用汉语 1500 高频词语表》等大量具有实用参考价值的附录。使用者可以根据实际教学情况，参考、选择并增加所需要的相关内容，制订出个性化的教学大纲或教材编写纲目。

2.3　针对性原则

针对国际汉语教学从专业化日益走向大众化、普及型、应用型的发展趋势，《大纲》在编写过程中，最大可能地兼顾到小学、中学及社会人士等不同使用对象的特点，最大限度地降低了汉语学习的难度，对目标等级也做了适当调整，突出汉语交际能力在培养语言综合运用能力中的地位，以适应国际汉语教学的实际情况。

2.4 通用性原则

《大纲》参照《国际汉语能力标准》以及《欧洲语言教学与评估框架性共同标准》等国际认可的语言能力标准，从跨文化语言教学的角度，吸收了现阶段国际汉语教学的成果与经验，对典型的汉语语言知识、文化知识等教学内容进行了梳理，并提供了具有可操作性的示例建议，以便于更多的国际汉语教学工作者在教学、师资培训、教材编写等方面参考使用。

3. 内 容

3.1 总目标

国际汉语教学课程的总目标是，使学习者在学习汉语语言知识与技能的同时，进一步强化学习目的，培养自主学习与合作学习的能力，形成有效的学习策略，最终具备语言综合运用能力。

语言综合运用能力由语言知识、语言技能、策略、文化意识四方面内容组成。其中语言知识和语言技能是语言综合运用能力的基础；策略是提高效率、促进学习者自主学习和发展自我能力的重要条件；文化意识则是培养学习者具备国际视野和多元文化意识，更得体地运用语言的必备元素。

上述四方面内容相互交叉渗透，环环相扣。如下图所示：

国际汉语教学课程目标结构关系图

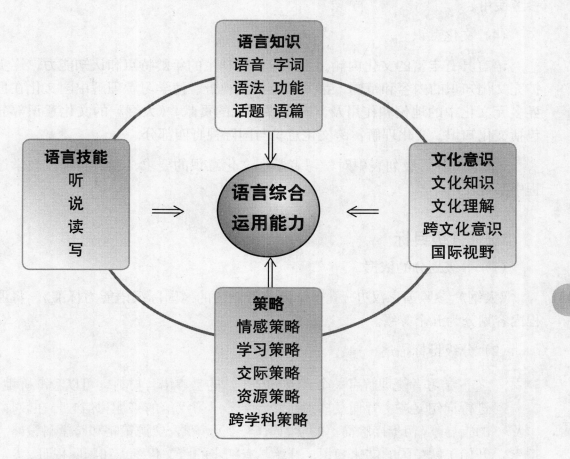

（1）语言知识

语言知识是语言综合运用能力的有机组成部分，是发展语言技能的重要基础。《大纲》从语音、字词、语法、功能、话题、语篇6个方面对语言知识进行了描述。

（2）语言技能

语言技能是语言综合运用能力的重要组成部分。《大纲》各等级所描述的语言技能包括对综合技能的运用，以及对听、说、读、写各单项技能的分级要求。

（3）策略

策略部分包括情感策略、学习策略（认知策略、元认知策略）、交际策略、资源策略和跨学科策略。

《大纲》各等级列表中对学习者掌握策略的要求，仅供教师在教学过程中参考使用。

（4）文化意识

语言具有丰富的文化内涵。教师应根据学生的年龄特点和认知能力，逐步扩充文化知识的内容和范围，帮助学生拓宽视野，使学习者理解中国文化在世界多元文化中的地位和作用及其对世界文化的贡献。《大纲》的文化意识部分包括文化知识、文化理解、跨文化意识与国际视野四部分。

《大纲》各等级列表中对学习者掌握文化意识的要求，仅供教师在教学过程中参考使用。

3.2 分级目标

（1）等级划分的依据

《大纲》参照国家汉办 / 孔子学院总部制定的《国际汉语能力标准》，将课程内容划分为五个等级。

（2）分级目标描述

一级	学习者能理解有关个人或日常生活的基本语言材料，可以较准确地进行词句复述、背诵及抄写。开始培养学习汉语的兴趣和信心。在教师的指导下，初步接触简单的学习策略、交际策略、资源策略和跨学科策略。开始了解中国的文化知识，开始具有初步的跨文化意识和国际视野。
二级	学习者能理解和掌握有关个人或日常生活的基本语言材料，掌握基本句型，可以造一些简单的句子，对事物作简单的描述，以比较简单的方式进行简单的语言交流。开始培养学习汉语的兴趣和信心。初步学习简单的学习策略、交际策略、资源策略和跨学科策略。开始了解中国的文化知识，具有初步的跨文化意识和国际视野。
三级	学习者能理解并学习与生活相关的语言材料，可以运用较为复杂的句型，就熟悉的话题进行沟通、交流与描述，可以组织简单的语段。具有学习汉语的兴趣和信心。掌握简单的学习策略、交际策略、资源策略和跨学科策略。了解简单的中国文化知识，具有一般跨文化意识和国际视野。

四级	学习者能理解与社会生活相关的语言材料，造句的正确率高，能就熟悉的题材进行描述、解释或比较，可以进行一些基本的成段表达，能组织简单的篇章。具有学习汉语的兴趣和信心。掌握一般的学习策略、交际策略、资源策略和跨学科策略。了解中国文化中基本的文化知识，具有基本的跨文化意识和国际视野。
五级	学习者能理解多种主题的语言材料，能熟练造句，掌握一些成段表达的技巧，具备组织比较完整的篇章的能力，具备进行比较流利的语言交流的能力。对学习汉语具有较强的兴趣和信心。较全面地掌握学习策略、交际策略、资源策略和跨学科策略。比较深入地了解中国的文化知识，具有跨文化意识和国际视野。

4.《大纲》的适用对象

　　《大纲》旨在为国际汉语教学工作者和汉语学习者提供服务。适用对象包括成年人与未成年人、在校学习者与社会学习者、有汉语背景者与无汉语背景者等。在校学习者包括公立及私立小学、中学（初、高中）、国际学校的学生及大学生等；社会学习者包括成人夜校、成人周末学校及汉语补习学校的学生。此外，《大纲》对中国的国际汉语教师及志愿者教师也具有参考价值，同时也为编写国际汉语教材提供了参考。

5.《大纲》的研制过程

　　自 2007 年初，国家汉办 / 孔子学院总部先后组织世界各地 300 多位汉语教学专家和教师，参与《大纲》的编写研制。加拿大、美国、英国、法国、澳大利亚、日本、韩国、德国、俄罗斯、哥伦比亚、新加坡等多个国家的中文教师协会、孔子学院、中文教学机构等协助完成了文献搜集、基础调研、意见反馈、文稿撰写及修改等工作，在此表示感谢。

　　《大纲》正文部分由冯睿（加拿大）翻译，附录一和附录二由张黎新翻译，附录三由彭琳翻译，附录四由范海祥翻译，附录五由吴晓波翻译，一并致谢。

　　由于时间较紧，调研不够，《大纲》尚有诸多不足之处，有待于在实施过程中日臻完善，欢迎广大读者提出宝贵意见。

国家汉办 / 孔子学院总部

2008 年 3 月

目 录

国际汉语教学通用课程大纲

第一章 一级目标及内容

一、目标

　　学习者能理解有关个人或日常生活的基本语言材料，可以较准确地进行词句复述、背诵及抄写。开始培养学习汉语的兴趣和信心。在教师的指导下，初步接触简单的学习策略、交际策略、资源策略和跨学科策略。开始了解中国的文化知识，开始具有初步的跨文化意识和国际视野。

二、语言知识

知　识	目　标　描　述
语音	1. 掌握汉语拼音的正确读音； 2. 初步识别汉字的发音； 3. 了解汉语是有声调的语言，汉语普通话有四个声调和轻声。
字词	在教师的指导下： 1. 掌握 150 个左右常用汉字，做到听、说、读、写四会； 2. 开始识别最基本的组字成分 / 部件或汉字的偏旁部首； 3. 了解汉字的基本笔画、笔顺； 4. 初步了解汉语中字与词的关系； 5. 初步掌握 300 个与日常生活、学校生活有关的最基本词汇。
语法	了解和掌握： 1. 基本语序； 2. 常用句型，一般疑问句和用"不"的否定句； 3. 常用名词、数词和量词； 4. 人称代词、指示代词； 5. 描述人和物的基本表达方式； 6. 常用动词、形容词和程度副词。
功能	1. 能了解问候、感谢、道歉、告别等常用交际功能； 2. 能借助肢体语言或实物等完成最基本的日常生活交际。

知识	目 标 描 述
话题	1. 掌握最基本最简单的交际用语； 2. 了解与个人密切相关的简单话题，如家庭、个人信息、爱好等； 3. 熟悉与日常生活密切相关的简单话题,如数字、时间、日期、货币等。
语篇	在教师的指导下： 1. 初步了解在语境中恰当使用句子进行成段表达的方法，了解汉语语篇的行文思路； 2. 学会抓主干，并尝试通过修饰和限定成分，理解简单句子的基本内涵； 3. 初步感知汉语和母语语篇行文思路的差异和共性； 4. 初步感知简单的中文修辞方法； 5. 初步理解或领会口语和书面语篇章所表达的简单的思想感情。

三、语言技能

技 能		技 能 描 述
综合技能		能理解最基本的、与个人和日常生活密切相关的简单而又十分有限的语言材料，有时需要借助肢体语言、实物和语言环境等。能初步了解人物的称谓。熟悉日常生活中的一些问候语，用有限的简单词语介绍自己或与他人沟通。
单项技能	听	能听懂个人和日常生活中所熟悉的、简短的、发音准确清晰的基本词句和简单的课堂指令，可以借助说话者的肢体语言或语言环境猜出其意图，并能做出相应的反应。其中包括： 1. 与个人和日常生活密切相关的十分有限的简短词句和话语； 2. 基本的数字； 3. 他人的简单问候、称呼用语； 4. 最基本的课堂指示话语和要求； 5. 他人的简单请求。

技 能		技 能 描 述
单项技能	说	能跟读、复述或背诵所学词句，能简单回答别人的问候，介绍个人最基本的信息，用简单的词语表达最基本的需求。需要时可以借助肢体语言和实物来表达。其中包括： 1. 能跟读、复述或背诵课堂上所学的词句，声调基本正确； 2. 能说出本人的基本信息； 3. 能主动问候他人或对他人的问候做出回应； 4. 能用简单的词语表达最基本的需求或指令； 5. 能表达最基本的请求或寻求帮助。
	读	能识别拼音和课堂所教授的最基本的汉字、词语、数字、个人信息等。其中包括： 1. 能识别拼音，并借助词典使用拼音查找汉字； 2. 能大体识别与个人及日常生活密切相关的简短信息类材料中的特定信息； 3. 能基本看懂一般社交场合中最常用的问候语和感谢语； 4. 能大体理解日常生活中最常见的字词和数字； 5. 能借助图片等大体理解最常见的、明显的指示语或标志。
	写	能模仿写出课堂所教授的规定的基本汉字，书写基本正确，能用拼音写出简单的词句。其中包括： 1. 能用正确的笔顺抄写汉字； 2. 能填写最基本的个人信息，如姓名、国籍等； 3. 能书写学过的最简单的日常生活用语和日期、时间、数字等； 4. 能正确书写社交场合中的简单用语，如贺卡上的祝福语等。

5

四、策略

策　略	目　标　描　述
情感策略	1. 初步培养学习汉语的愿望和兴趣； 2. 初步培养学习汉语的自信心，使学习者主动使用汉语； 3. 克服犯错误时的沮丧情绪。
学习策略	1. 掌握简单的项目分类； 2. 初步培养自己的模仿能力； 3. 初步学习用已有的知识学习新的语言知识； 4. 能将孤立的字词组成简单的句子； 5. 初步学习听取他人意见，以改进自己学习中出现的问题； 6. 初步学会制订自己的学习计划； 7. 初步学习遇到困难时寻求帮助的方法。
交际策略	1. 运用简单的情感策略，提高学习效率，观察他人的动作并会模仿； 2. 在教师的指导下，在课内与同学和老师进行简单的交流，了解并遵守汉语交际的基本礼仪； 3. 在教师的帮助下，借助手势和表情等非语言手段，逐步提高语言交际的能力。
资源策略	1. 在教师的指导下，开始使用教科书、图片、图解字典和多媒体资源，查找所需信息和资料； 2. 在教师的指导下，开始通过教师和同学获取学习的资源。
跨学科策略	1. 在教师的指导下，开始初步重视自己知识面的拓展，并能初步认识到学习中国语言和文化对各学科学习的帮助； 2. 初步认识各学科知识对学习中国语言和文化的帮助并初步意识到培养综合能力的重要性； 3. 本级跨学科范围包括音乐、美术、历史、民俗等。

五、文化意识

文化意识	目 标 描 述
文化知识	1. 初步了解所在国有关个人使用不同语言的好处； 2. 初步了解所在国和中国在文化、教育等方面的发展及成就； 3. 初步体验中国文化中的物质文化部分，如食品、服装等； 4. 初步了解简单的汉语故事、典故中的文化内涵； 5. 初步了解中国文化中的语言交际功能和非语言交际功能； 6. 初步了解中国的简单交际礼仪与习俗； 7. 初步了解中国文化中的人际关系。
文化理解	1. 逐渐对中国文化产生兴趣； 2. 初步体验中国文化最基本的组成部分，了解语言学习与文化的关系； 3. 接触中国文化中最基本的价值观念； 4. 接触文化的多元性和相互渗透性。
跨文化意识	1. 开始思考有关中国文化和所在国文化的共性和差异； 2. 通过学习中国文化，开始理解培养跨文化意识的重要性。
国际视野	1. 开始初步接触中国和所在国的一些文化现象； 2. 通过学习汉语语言文化，开始初步思考从不同视角看世界的重要性； 3. 接触最初步的世界公民意识。

第二章 二级目标及内容

一、目标

学习者能理解和掌握有关个人或日常生活的基本语言材料,掌握基本句型,可以造一些简单的句子,对事物作简单的描述,以比较简单的方式进行简单的语言交流。开始培养学习汉语的兴趣和信心。初步学习简单的学习策略、交际策略、资源策略和跨学科策略。开始了解中国的文化知识,具有初步的跨文化意识和国际视野。

二、语言知识

知 识	目 标 描 述
语音	1. 了解语音在汉语学习中的意义; 2. 初步掌握汉语的几种常见变调规则; 3. 在日常会话中基本做到语音、语调正确。
字词	1. 掌握 300 个左右的常用汉字,做到听、说、读、写四会; 2. 初步辨别字音、字形、字义; 3. 了解汉字与词的关系; 4. 学习约 600 个左右与日常生活、学校生活有关的基本词汇。
语法	了解和掌握: 1. 人民币、钱数和疑问代词; 2. 时间、地点、方位的基本表达方式; 3. 特殊疑问句; 4. 定语、状语的基本结构和功能; 5. 表示存在的方式; 6. 表示意愿的方式。
功能	1. 能运用问候、感谢、道歉、告别等常用交际功能; 2. 能了解和简单运用询问、介绍、说明等交际功能; 3. 能完成简单的日常生活交际。

知 识	目 标 描 述
话题	1. 熟悉与个人、家庭密切相关的一些话题； 2. 熟悉与日常生活、兴趣爱好等相关的话题； 3. 初步了解与校园生活或职业工作相关的简单话题。
语篇	1. 在教师的指导下，初步了解在语境中恰当使用句子进行成段表达的方法； 2. 在教师的指导下，在抓主干的同时，初步通过修饰、限定成分，理解句子的基本内涵； 3. 在教师的指导下，感知中文和母语语篇行文思路的差异和共性； 4. 在教师的指导下，感知较简单的修辞方法，如夸张、排比等； 5. 在教师的指导下，初步理解或领会口语和书面语篇章所表达的一般思想感情。

三、语言技能

技 能		技 能 描 述
综合技能		能基本理解熟悉的、与个人和日常生活密切相关的简单语言材料，并能就这些常见话题以较简单的方式与他人沟通，介绍自己或他人的基本情况。初步了解生活中表达情感（感谢、道歉）及态度（肯定或否定）的简单词语，了解不同场合的问候及告别方式。
单项技能	听	能基本理解与个人和日常生活密切相关的基本语言材料，捕捉相关信息，能听懂教师课堂用语和要求，并根据需要进行简单的操作。其中包括： 1. 与个人和日常生活密切相关的简短谈话中的相关信息； 2. 日常生活中不同场合下常见的简单词句和问候； 3. 与个人和日常生活密切相关的简短谈话中的提问、回答、要求或请求，理解对方的态度和情感； 4. 交谈中涉及到的数字、时间、地点等具体信息； 5. 课堂上的指示用语。

技　能		技　能　描　述
单项技能	说	句调准确，能模仿造句，就提出的问题做出简单的回答，并就日常生活中所熟悉的话题与他人沟通，能表达基本的个人需求。其中包括： 1. 能用简单的词语介绍自己或他人的基本情况； 2. 能用简单的词句就日常生活中非常熟悉的话题与他人沟通，提出简单问题或给出明确的回答； 3. 能在熟悉的情境下，用学过的词语与他人沟通，给出简单的指示或要求，表达需求和寻求帮助； 4. 能在不同的场合下恰当地表达态度和情感。
	读	能认读规定的基本汉字、词句及简短的文字材料，看懂学习要求，并能从简短的文字材料中获取相关信息。其中包括： 1. 能识别个人和日常生活中常见的简短信息类材料中的主要信息； 2. 能基本认读和理解常见社交场合表示问候、感谢或邀请类的简短材料； 3. 能猜测含有熟悉字词的日常生活中的一些标识及简单说明性材料的内容； 4. 能大体看懂简单的便条、通知或表格； 5. 能在格式固定、清楚熟悉的简短材料中查找到特定信息。
	写	能默写规定的基本汉字，掌握笔画和笔顺，能写出一些自己造的句子。其中包括： 1. 能用简单的词语填写、表达与个人生活密切相关的信息； 2. 能用简单的词语或句子表达感谢、道歉、祝贺、告别等简单信息； 3. 能记录、填写或抄写与家庭或个人生活密切相关的基本信息； 4. 能用书面的形式简短回答与个人生活密切相关的简单问题。

四、策略

策　略	目　标　描　述
情感策略	1. 增强学习汉语的兴趣，多主动参与有助于提高汉语能力的活动； 2. 增强学习汉语的自信心，愿意主动使用汉语交流与表达； 3. 学习克服语言学习中焦虑情绪的方法。
学习策略	1. 体验汉语学习，能够集中精力接受语言输入； 2. 初步接受汉语语言学习与习得的方式； 3. 借助想象获取及记住新的信息，利用形象思维和发散性思维达到理想的学习效果； 4. 能将孤立的字词组成较简单的句子，能将较简单的视觉形式信息转化成较简单的语言形式的信息； 5. 适应学习环境，自觉听取他人意见，以解决自己学习中出现的问题； 6. 在教师的指导下，开始形成自己的学习方法并学习如何制订学习计划； 7. 初步掌握预习和复习的方法； 8. 学会创造和选择学习环境。
交际策略	1. 运用简单的情感策略提高学习效率，并能寻求他人的帮助； 2. 在课内外与教师、朋友进行交流； 3. 在教师的帮助下，借助手势和表情等非语言手段提高语言交际能力，开始遵守汉语交际的基本礼仪。
资源策略	1. 在教师的的指导下，开始使用教科书、图解字典和词典，并利用图书馆、网上等多种资源，查找所需信息和资料； 2. 通过老师、同学、学校和社区获取语言学习的资源。
跨学科策略	1. 开始初步重视自己知识面的拓展； 2. 初步认识到学习中国语言和文化对各学科学习的促进作用； 3. 初步认识到各学科知识对学习中国语言和文化的促进作用； 4. 初步理解掌握综合能力的重要性； 5. 本级跨学科范围包括历史、民俗、艺术等。

11

五、文化意识

文化意识	目 标 描 述
文化知识	1. 初步接触所在国有关个人使用不同语言的权利； 2. 初步了解所在国和中国在文化、教育等方面的发展及成就； 3. 初步体验中国文化、艺术、节日庆祝等； 4. 初步了解汉语中最常见的简单成语故事、某些典故的文化内涵； 5. 初步了解中国文化中的语言交际和非语言交际功能； 6. 初步了解中国的简单交际礼仪与习俗； 7. 初步了解中国文化中的人际关系； 8. 初步了解华人对所在国社会的贡献。
文化理解	1. 开始了解文化不仅可以习得，而且可以通过学习语言获得； 2. 开始了解文化学习和语言学习的关系：语言是文化的重要组成部分； 3. 开始初步了解中国文化中的基本价值观念； 4. 体验文化的多元性、动态性和相互渗透性。
跨文化意识	1. 初步思考有关中国文化和所在国文化的共性和差异； 2. 通过学习中国文化，进一步理解跨文化意识的重要性； 3. 通过对所在国文化与中国文化的对比，开始对所在国某些文化现象进行初步的客观思考。
国际视野	1. 通过学习汉语，开始初步思考拓展国际视野的重要性； 2. 通过学习中国文化，开始初步考虑从不同的视角看世界的重要性； 3. 具有初步的世界公民意识。

第三章 三级目标及内容

一、目标

学习者能理解并学习与生活相关的语言材料，可以运用较为复杂的句型，就熟悉的话题进行沟通、交流与描述，可以组织简单的语段。具有学习汉语的兴趣和信心。掌握简单的学习策略、交际策略、资源策略和跨学科策略。了解简单的中国文化知识，具有一般跨文化意识和国际视野。

二、语言知识

知 识	目 标 描 述
语音	1. 对汉语拼音知识有一定的了解； 2. 能根据拼音拼读出不熟悉的生词和句子； 3. 在日常会话中能听懂带有连读、变调等语流音变因素的话语； 4. 在日常会话中做到语音、语调基本正确。
字词	1. 掌握 450 个左右常用汉字，做到听、说、读、写四会； 2. 了解组字成分 / 部件 / 汉字的偏旁部首； 3. 进一步辨识字音、字形、字义； 4. 能基本正确理解话语中的词汇意义； 5. 能得体地运用学过的词汇进行表达； 6. 学会约 900 个与日常生活、学习、工作有关的词语。
语法	了解和掌握： 1. 常用能愿动词、介词； 2. 基本比较句； 3. 描述事件或行为正在进行的表达方式； 4. 助词"了"的基本用法； 5. 用"没有"的否定句。

知 识	目 标 描 述
功能	1. 能根据不同的情境恰当地运用熟悉的交际功能项目； 2. 能了解和简单表达说明、叙述、描述等交际功能； 3. 能完成一般日常生活和简单的学习、工作等领域的交际。
话题	1. 进一步熟悉有关日常生活、兴趣爱好等方面的话题； 2. 初步了解个人周围环境、学习、工作等方面的话题； 3. 了解有关中国的比较简单的一般社会生活和文化方面的话题。
语篇	1. 接触汉语和母语语篇行文思路的差异和共性； 2. 在教师的指导下，在抓主干的同时，初步通过修饰、限定成分，理解句子的内涵； 3. 尝试运用简单的中文修辞方法，感知比较复杂的中文修辞方法； 4. 根据比较简单的修辞方法的特征和功能，初步学习口语和书面语篇章所表达的思想感情。

14

三、语言技能

技 能		技 能 描 述
综合 技能		能理解与日常生活和学习相关、并在一般交际场合中经常遇到的最基本的语言材料。能就熟悉的话题与他人进行沟通和交流，并就这些话题组织简单的语段。初步具备借助重音、停顿、语调或肢体语言等手段来提高交际效果的基本能力。
单 项 技 能	听	能听懂日常生活和学习中简单的交谈或讲述，听懂常见的交际性话语或要求，初步满足生活和学习的基本需求。其中包括： 1. 能明白日常生活、学校生活中的交谈或简短发言的大意，听懂谈话或发言中的基本信息； 2. 能抓住交谈中重点提示的词句和话语； 3. 听懂与个人生活和经历有关的简短会话或交谈； 4. 听懂一般常识性的简单且直接的问题； 5. 捕捉到闲谈、一般性介绍或电话交谈中的一些基本信息； 6. 理解简单故事的梗概。

技　能		技　能　描　述
单项技能	说	能参与简单的对话，基本表达个人的观点和需求，模仿造一些稍微复杂的句子，能对熟悉的事物和生活中发生的一些事情做简单的陈述。其中包括： 1. 学会使用重音、停顿、语调或肢体语言等手段来加强语气； 2. 参与简单或日常的对话，谈论个人需求； 3. 能就日常生活及学习中熟悉的话题与他人进行简单的交流，或做简单陈述； 4. 能简单描述个人或日常生活中常见的事物、活动或一段个人经历； 5. 能对日常生活中的一些事物做出明确的表态，并能简单描述某一现象或状况； 6. 能讲述简短的故事。
	读	能阅读日常生活或学习中常见的简短书面材料，了解大意，识别基本信息；能在题材熟悉的段落中找到所需的特定信息。其中包括： 1. 能阅读日常生活或学习中常见的简短书面材料，了解大意，识别基本信息； 2. 能读懂简单社交场合中的留言、记录、电子邮件或简短信函； 3. 能看懂日常生活中简短的介绍性或说明性材料； 4. 能读懂与日常生活密切相关的、内容可预测的简单叙述性或描写性材料，能抓住主要信息； 5. 能在内容熟悉的题材中快速找到所需的特定信息。
	写	能用简单的词语填写或描述与个人生活密切相关的信息；能用最基本的词语或句子就一般场合下熟悉的话题进行简单的书面交流；能组织简单的段落。其中包括： 1. 能用简单的词语填写、回答或介绍与个人生活密切相关的信息； 2. 能用最基本的词语或句子就一般场合下熟悉的话题进行简单的书面交流； 3. 能就一般社交场合下熟悉的话题书写简短的信息； 4. 能记录、抄写或填写事实性或说明性信息； 5. 能组织简单的段落叙述或描述个人生活、家庭生活及学习生活； 6. 能编写小故事、撰写简单的计划等。

15

四、策略

策略	目标描述
情感策略	1. 明确学习动机，了解学习目的是为了沟通与表达； 2. 努力克服困难，愿意主动向他人求教； 3. 理解学习汉语对社会、家庭和个人所带来的利益； 4. 对汉语、中国文化以及世界文化产生较积极的情感； 5. 提高汉语学习的积极性并力争取得与其水平相当的成绩； 6. 掌握自我鼓励的方法。
学习策略	1. 通过批判性思维方式获取信息； 2. 借助肢体语言加强记忆； 3. 初步掌握做笔记的方法，并养成做笔记的习惯； 4. 初步明确学习需要和学习兴趣； 5. 能将孤立的字词组成较复杂的描述性句子； 6. 能将视觉形式的信息转化成语言形式的信息； 7. 能对前后学习内容进行纵向的梳理； 8. 能积极听取他人意见，以解决自己学习中出现的问题； 9. 在教师的指导下，认识自己的学习方法并学习如何制订学习计划； 10. 在教师的指导下，拟定更进一步的学习计划； 11. 初步掌握自我监控的学习过程； 12. 寻求适应自己的学习方法。
交际策略	1. 在教师的指导下，开始与教师和同学进行交流； 2. 开始意识到交际中的语言障碍，并积极寻求克服的方法； 3. 开始借助手势和表情等非语言手段，提高语言交际效率； 4. 在教师的指导下，体验遵守汉语交际的基本礼仪； 5. 积极参与小组活动。
资源策略	1. 在教师的指导下，开始使用教科书、图解字典、词典和多媒体资源，并利用图书馆、互联网等多种资源，查找所需信息和资料； 2. 通过老师、同学、朋友、学校、社区和工作环境获取语言学习的资源。

策 略	目 标 描 述
跨学科策略	1. 重视自己知识面的拓展； 2. 认识学习中国语言和文化对学习各学科知识的促进作用； 3. 认识各学科知识对学习中国语言和文化的帮助；能在教师的指导下，运用所学知识和技能学习中国语言和文化； 4. 理解个人综合能力的重要性，并在教师的指导下，有意识地培养自己的综合能力； 5. 本级跨学科范围包括历史、艺术、民俗等。

五、文化意识

文化意识	目 标 描 述
文化知识	1. 开始学习所在国有关个人和社区学习不同语言的权利； 2. 开始了解所在国和中国在文化、教育等方面的发展及成就； 3. 开始学习中国文化、艺术等方面的历史及其对世界文化的贡献； 4. 开始了解汉语语言文化的发展历史及其对世界文化的贡献； 5. 基本了解汉语中最常用的成语故事和典故的文化内涵； 6. 开始了解汉语文化中的语言交际和非语言交际功能； 7. 开始了解中国的交际礼仪与习俗； 8. 开始了解汉语文化中的社会结构和人际关系，如个人、家庭等； 9. 开始了解华人对所在国社会的贡献。
文化理解	1. 开始理解文化不仅可以习得，而且可以通过学习获得； 2. 开始理解文化学习和语言学习的关系：语言是文化的重要组成部分； 3. 基本了解中国文化中的基本价值观念； 4. 开始理解文化的多元性、动态性和相互渗透性。

文化意识	目 标 描 述
跨文化意识	1. 初步了解有关中国文化和所在国文化的共性和差异； 2. 通过学习中国文化，开始初步培养自身的跨文化意识； 3. 通过对所在国文化和中国文化的对比，开始对所在国文化习俗和思维习惯进行客观的评价。
国际视野	1. 通过学习汉语，开始初步了解世界文化，拓展国际视野； 2. 通过学习汉语语言文化，开始初步培养从不同视角解释世界多元现象的能力； 3. 具有初步的世界公民意识。

第四章 四级目标及内容

一、目标

　　学习者能理解与社会生活相关的语言材料，造句的正确率高，能就熟悉的题材进行描述、解释或比较，可以进行一些基本的成段表达，能组织简单的篇章。具有学习汉语的兴趣和信心。掌握一般的学习策略、交际策略、资源策略和跨学科策略。了解中国文化中基本的文化知识，具有基本的跨文化意识和国际视野。

二、语言知识

知　识	目　标　描　述
语音	1. 掌握汉语的拼音系统； 2. 能根据语音、语调、重音等了解话语含义； 3. 在日常会话中声调基本正确，并能正确使用连读、变调等； 4. 在日常会话中做到语音、语调基本正确、自然。
字词	1. 掌握 600 个左右常用汉字，做到听、说、读、写四会； 2. 了解一些复杂的汉字结构规则； 3. 基本具备辨别字形、辨识字音、理解字义的能力； 4. 能简单了解汉语词语的结构规律； 5. 学会扩展使用约 1200 个左右与社会、生活、工作、学习等相关的常用词语。
语法	了解和掌握： 1. 时间副词； 2. 助词"过"的用法； 3. 时量补语、动量补语； 4. "是……的"句的用法； 5. 兼语句； 6. 常用复句。

知 识	目 标 描 述
功能	1. 能得体地运用熟悉的交际功能项目； 2. 能有效地表达情感、态度和意见等； 3. 能完成学习、工作及社交等领域的交际。
话题	1. 进一步熟悉社会生活方面的话题； 2. 了解有关风俗习惯、科学文化和文学艺术等方面的话题； 3. 了解当代中国和世界的热点话题。
语篇	1. 体验中文和母语语篇行文思路的差异和共性； 2. 在抓主干的同时，掌握通过修饰、限定成分，理解句子内涵的方法； 3. 尝试运用简单和比较复杂的中文修辞方法，感知复杂的中文修辞方法； 4. 根据比较复杂的修辞方法的特征和功能，理解口语和书面语篇章所表达的思想感情。

20

三、语言技能

技 能		技 能 描 述
综合技能		能理解工作或社交场合中比较简单、内容熟悉的语言材料，抓住重点，把握细节。能就熟悉的话题与他人进行交流，表述基本清楚，且有一定的连贯性；会使用基本的交际策略。能描述自己的一些经历，表达自己的一些看法，给出简单的理由或解释。
单项技能	听	能听懂工作场合及社交场合中的谈话或发言，理解陈述性或论述性表达的大意，抓住主要内容和关键信息。其中包括： 1. 能抓住工作场合中话题熟悉的谈话或发言的主要内容和观点； 2. 能抓住社交场合中对话或交谈的主要内容和关键信息，领悟说话人的真实意图； 3. 能大致听懂与个人或工作相关的一些议论； 4. 能理解陈述性或论述性话语的大意； 5. 能听懂与常见话题相关的一系列指示或要求； 6. 能听懂稍长的叙述性故事。

技 能		技 能 描 述
单项技能	说	能在工作及社交场合与人沟通，就一般性话题与人进行交谈或发表看法，能清楚地表达个人的观点，表述具有一定的连贯性。其中包括： 1. 能在一般社交场合与他人沟通，就一般性话题进行交谈； 2. 能参与简单的讨论，清楚地表达自己的观点； 3. 能就某件事提出建议或意见，并能给出理由； 4. 能使用基本的交际策略，表述基本清楚，且有一定的连贯性； 5. 能处理简单的日常事务，做出指示或安排； 6. 能较为完整地叙述或报告某件事情的经过或情况。
	读	能看懂日常生活、学习、工作中较为浅显的介绍性、说明性、叙述性文字，理解其主要意思和关键信息。其中包括： 1. 能看懂一般场合中浅显的材料，抓住主要内容和关键信息； 2. 能读懂工作及社交中的普通信函、电子邮件、通知等文字材料； 3. 能看懂日常生活中普通的介绍性或说明性材料； 4. 能读懂一般场合中语言浅显、话题熟悉的描述性或叙述性短文，能抓住中心议题，抓住某些重要细节，领悟作者的真实意图； 5. 能阅读大部分内容为事实性信息的篇章，从中找到所需的特定信息。
	写	能就基本的日常学习、工作或社交话题进行描述，能按一定格式书写简短的篇章，传递或表达恰当的信息。其中包括： 1. 能根据所读或所听材料做简单的记录，概括出大意； 2. 能就个人经历或熟悉的有关学习、工作或社交话题做简单的成段描述，语句基本通顺，表达基本清楚； 3. 能填写简单的工作表格和计划书等； 4. 能根据简短的口头报告或参考资料整理出简单的笔记； 5. 能在两事物之间进行对比描述； 6. 能撰写日记，语句基本通顺，表达基本清楚，且具有一定的连贯性。

四、策略

策　略	目　标　描　述
情感策略	1. 能全面并正确地认识学习汉语的意义； 2. 加强合作精神，愿意与他人分享各种学习资源； 3. 培养学好汉语的毅力和克服困难的意志； 4. 培养、调整与加强学习汉语的动机和态度； 5. 对汉语、中国文化以及世界文化有积极的情感。
学习策略	1. 能就熟悉的话题，找出研究课题，进行初步研究； 2. 能写简单的个人日志； 3. 能预习学习内容； 4. 能将视觉形式信息转化成相应复杂的语言形式信息； 5. 能对前后学习内容进行纵向梳理和简单的横向比较分析； 6. 主动参与学习过程中的各项任务； 7. 营造学习环境，征求他人意见，以解决自己学习中出现的问题； 8. 能在教师的指导下，制订自己的学习计划，加强自己薄弱项目的学习。
交际策略	1. 在教师的指导下，运用情感策略参加学生的课堂互动活动； 2. 意识到自己在交际中的语言障碍并开始克服； 3. 在课内外能积极主动地与他人交流，包括教师、同学等； 4. 借助手势和表情等非语言手段，提高语言交际效果； 5. 在真实交际中学习遵守汉语交际的基本礼仪； 6. 乐于主动分享自己学习中成功的经验及失败的教训。
资源策略	1. 接触各项信息，可以分辨事实与观点； 2. 使用教科书，图解字典和词典，并利用图书馆、互联网和报纸等多种资源，查找所需信息和资料； 3. 能比较自觉地通过老师、同学、朋友、学校、社区和工作环境获取语言学习的资源。

策　略	目　标　描　述
跨学科策略	1. 重视自己知识面的拓展； 2. 较深刻地认识学习中国语言和文化对学习各学科知识的帮助和促进作用； 3. 较深刻地认识各学科知识对学习中国语言和文化的帮助，并在教师的指导下，运用所学知识和技能学习中国语言和文化； 4. 理解个人综合能力的重要性，并有意识地培养自己的综合能力； 5. 本级跨学科范围包括历史、艺术、民俗、地理、政治、经济、交通等。

五、文化意识

23

文化意识	目　标　描　述
文化知识	1. 基本了解所在国个人及群体学习不同语言的权利； 2. 基本了解所在国个人、社区和社会使用不同语言的权利； 3. 基本了解所在国和中国在经济、文化、科学、教育等方面的发展、交流及成就； 4. 基本了解中国文学、艺术、科学、思想等方面的成就及其对世界文化的贡献； 5. 基本了解汉语言文化的发展及其在世界文化中的地位、贡献和作用； 6. 进一步了解汉语中常用成语、俗语、某些典故的文化内涵； 7. 基本了解汉语言文化中的语言交际和非语言交际功能； 8. 基本了解汉语言文化中的交际礼仪与习俗； 9. 基本了解汉语言文化中的社会结构和人际关系； 10. 基本了解所在国华人的创业史和华人对所在国社会的贡献。

文化意识	目 标 描 述
文化理解	1. 理解文化不仅可以习得，而且可以通过学习获得； 2. 理解文化学习和语言学习的关系：语言是文化的重要组成部分； 3. 基本理解中国文化中的价值观念； 4. 基本理解文化的多元性、动态性和相互渗透性； 5. 初步具有运用批判思维方式学习、了解有关中国文化和所在国文化的能力。
跨文化意识	1. 基本了解有关中国文化和所在国文化的共性和差异； 2. 通过学习中国文化，进一步培养跨文化意识； 3. 通过对所在国文化与汉语文化的对比，加深对所在国文化习俗和思维习惯的客观认识。
国际视野	1. 通过学习汉语，初步了解世界文化，拓展国际视野； 2. 通过学习汉语言文化，初步培养从不同视角解释世界多元现象的能力； 3. 同时具有民族认同感和世界认同感； 4. 通过文化学习，拓宽思维和视野； 5. 培养世界公民意识。

第五章　五级目标及内容

一、目标

　　学习者能理解多种主题的语言材料,能熟练造句,掌握一些成段表达的技巧,具备组织比较完整的篇章的能力,具备进行比较流利的语言交流的能力。对学习汉语具有较强的兴趣和信心。较全面地掌握学习策略、交际策略、资源策略和跨学科策略。比较深入地了解中国的文化知识,具有跨文化意识和国际视野。

二、语言知识

知　识	目　标　描　述
语音	1. 在日常交际中,逐步做到语音、语调自然、流畅; 2. 能运用语音、语调、重音等手段表达特殊含义; 3. 初步了解汉语的节奏和韵律; 4. 能听懂略带不同口音的普通话。
字词	1. 掌握 800 个左右常用汉字,做到听、说、读、写四会; 2. 基本掌握汉字的构形规律; 3. 音、形、义运用基本正确; 4. 在自己熟悉的话题范围内,能选择合适的词语进行交流或表达; 5. 了解汉语词汇的词义变化及日常生活中新出现的词汇,能使用约 1500 个左右的常用词语。
语法	了解和掌握: 1. 结果补语、趋向补语、可能补语、程度补语; 2. "把"字句; 3. 汉语被动意义的表达方式; 4. 各种复句。
功能	1. 能综合运用熟悉的交际功能项目; 2. 能根据交流的需要,进一步学习并掌握新的语言表达形式和交际功能; 3. 能完成工作、社交和相关专业领域的交际。

知识	目 标 描 述
话题	1. 进一步熟悉当代中国和世界的热点话题； 2. 能综合运用已经掌握的话题内容。
语篇	1. 体验中文和母语语篇行文思路的差异和共性； 2. 在抓主干的同时，通过修饰、限定成分，理解句子的内涵； 3. 掌握简单、比较复杂和复杂的修辞方法，感知更复杂的中文修辞方法； 4. 根据汉语普通修辞方法的特征和功能，基本理解口语和书面语篇章所表达的思想感情。

三、语言技能

技 能		技 能 描 述
综合技能		能理解多种场合下的多种主题的稍复杂的语言材料，包括与个人工作和专业相关的语言材料，能够把握重点，进行初步概括和分析。能使用一些交际策略参与谈话，包括专业领域内的一般性话题的交流和讨论，表明自己的观点和态度，并能了解各种意见。初步体验汉语的方言及地区性差异，熟悉一些简单的成语和俗语的文化含义。
单项技能	听	能听懂多种场合下稍复杂的谈话或发言，包括与自己的工作或专业相关的一般性谈论，能抓住要点，把握基本事实，明白说话人的目的和意图。其中包括： 1. 听懂多种社交或工作环境中稍复杂的交际用语和工作用语； 2. 听懂与自己工作或专业相关的讨论或发言，能抓住要点，把握基本事实，明白说话人的观点和论据； 3. 听懂话题熟悉、内容稍复杂的讲话或发言，抓住重点并掌握细节； 4. 听懂有关技术性或任务性的简单说明或讲解； 5. 理解一些成语、俗语的意思，领悟他人话语中暗含的意思； 6. 听懂略带口音的话题熟悉的普通话。

技 能		技 能 描 述
单项技能	说	能就一般性话题进行论述或参与讨论、争论，能清楚地陈述理由，表明观点和态度，能就某些特定的话题，如与工作或专业有关的话题进行进一步的讨论。其中包括： 1. 在多种场合下与他人就一般性话题进行有效的沟通和交流； 2. 就自己感兴趣的话题进行描述或论证，表达条理清晰，话语连贯； 3. 就一些特定话题与他人进行较为深入的交谈； 4. 参与讨论或争论，能清楚地陈述自己的观点，反驳别人的观点。
	读	能看懂有一定长度的较为复杂的语言材料，抓住大意，掌握重要事实和细节，把握篇章的结构。其中包括： 1. 读懂有一定长度的论述性材料，抓住大意，掌握重要事实和细节，把握文章的结构； 2. 读懂有一定长度的，带有一些成语、俗语、比喻的叙述性文章，准确理解其含义； 3. 大致看懂带有一些生词和术语的介绍性或说明性材料，掌握梗概并从中找到所需要的特定信息； 4. 能阅读一些与工作、学习、生活有关的浅显的科普文章。
	写	能就特定的话题进行描述、记录或说明，撰写相关的文件或文章，语句通顺；能正确反映客观情况，准确地表达自己的观点。其中包括： 1. 在口头交际的基础上，就一些特定话题与他人进行书面交流； 2. 表达个人的意见与看法，所写言之有物，语句通顺，语篇连贯； 3. 会写一般应用文或一定工作范围内的工作文件，格式基本正确，语言表达清楚； 4. 能就所听或所读的材料进行总结，有条理地写出摘要或简要报告； 5. 能撰写简短的一般性文章，就某些具体或抽象话题进行描述、阐释或说明，用词恰当，表达通顺，能正确反映事实，清楚地表达自己的观点。

四、策略

策 略	目 标 描 述
情感策略	1. 在汉语交流中能理解并尊重他人的情感； 2. 能在交流中用汉语表达自己的情感、态度和价值观； 3. 提高并保持汉语学习的动力并取得与其水平相当的成绩； 4. 以多角度看待自己在世界发展中的位置； 5. 乐于参与各种活动，主动培养自己对汉语和中国文化的兴趣和良好的学习习惯。
学习策略	1. 就熟悉的话题，找出研究课题进行进一步研究； 2. 在学习中，善于抓住重点； 3. 能对所学内容进行归纳和整理； 4. 理解学习汉语的价值，主动培养自学汉语的兴趣； 5. 能将视觉形式的信息转化成复杂语言形式的信息； 6. 能对前后学习内容进行纵向梳理和横向比较分析； 7. 积极营造学习环境，主动征求他人意见，以解决自己学习中出现的问题； 8. 基本了解自己的认知智能，有效调控自己的学习策略，增强学习效果，对自己的学习、计划、监控和评估负责； 9. 反思、检查学习目标、进度、过程及采用的策略。
交际策略	1. 在教师的指导下，运用情感策略主动参加课堂互动活动； 2. 在教师的指导下，运用解释或重复等方式克服交际中的语言障碍； 3. 能比较自如地与他人在课内外进行交流； 4. 有效地借助手势和表情等非语言手段提高交际效果； 5. 真实交际中逐渐注意并遵守汉语交际的基本礼仪； 6. 乐于与他人交流学习经验。
资源策略	1. 接触各种信息，可以分辨事实与观点； 2. 能比较熟练地通过教科书、字典、词典、报纸和杂志，并利用图书馆、互联网等多种资源查找所需信息和资料。

策　略	目　标　描　述
跨学科策略	1. 重视自己知识面的拓展。初步具备跨学科知识，初步做到触类旁通； 2. 能较熟练地将不同学科的知识贯通于中国语言和文化的学习之中； 3. 能较熟练地将所学的中国语言与文化知识贯通于不同学科的学习之中； 4. 初步具有比较全面的综合能力； 5. 本级跨学科范围包括：历史、艺术、民俗、地理、政治、经济、交通、文学、哲学等。

五、文化意识

文化意识	目　标　描　述
文化知识	1. 了解所在国个人及群体学习不同语言的权利； 2. 了解所在国个人、社区和社会使用不同语言的权利； 3. 了解所在国和中国在经济、文化、科学、教育等方面的发展、交流及成就； 4. 了解中国文学、艺术、科学、思想等方面的成就及其对世界文化的贡献； 5. 了解汉语语言文化的发展及其在世界文化大家庭中的地位、贡献和作用； 6. 了解汉语中常用成语、俗语和某些典故的文化内涵； 7. 了解汉语文化中的语言交际和非语言交际的功能； 8. 了解汉语文化中的交际礼仪与习俗； 9. 了解汉语文化中的社会结构和人际关系； 10. 了解中国的某些文化现象并具有对其进行解释的能力； 11. 了解所在国华人的创业史和华人对所在国社会的贡献。

文化意识	目 标 描 述
文化理解	1. 进一步理解文化不仅可以习得，而且可以通过学习获得； 2. 全面理解文化学习和语言学习的关系：语言是文化的重要组成部分； 3. 了解中国文化中的价值观念； 4. 了解文化的多元性、动态性和相互渗透性； 5. 学会运用批判性思维方式学习，了解有关中国文化和所在国文化的能力。
跨文化意识	1. 了解有关中国文化和所在国文化的共性和差异； 2. 通过学习中国文化，培养跨文化意识； 3. 通过对所在国文化与汉语文化的对比，加深对所在国文化习俗和思维习惯的客观认识。
国际视野	1. 通过学习汉语，了解世界文化，拓展国际视野； 2. 初步了解汉语的文化现象和渊源； 3. 通过学习汉语言文化，培养从不同视角对世界多元解释的能力； 4. 通过文化学习，拓宽思维和视野，培养由不同文化因素所达成的思维整合； 5. 了解中国与所在国的文化与渊源； 6. 培养较强的世界公民意识。

附录一 汉语教学话题及内容建议表

本表的编写目的是提供一些话题内容，供教师和教材编写者参考选用。由于语言具有相关性，每部分所涉及的内容有部分重复，使用者可以参照话题内容自行发挥，其中大部分话题可通用，也可以在不同等级内重复使用，循环上升。

话　题	内　容　建　议
个人信息	姓名，年龄，年级，出生地，生日，电话，地址，联系方式，家庭介绍，学校生活，工作生活，职业，邻里环境，语言，爱好，文化程度，家乡等
情感与态度	喜欢，不喜欢，高兴，不高兴，同意，不同意，满意，不满意，能够，不能够，可能，不可能，表扬，鼓励，感谢，遗憾，反感，抵触，焦虑，幽默，信任，怀疑，惊奇，忧伤，同情，害怕，担心，生气，抱怨等
社会交往	打招呼，问候，寒暄，介绍，交换名片，感谢，告别，邀请，拒绝，拜访，请求，建议，通知，允许，帮助，沟通，调解，祝愿与祝贺，聚会，约会，聚餐，打电话，发电子邮件，网络聊天，交际习俗与礼仪，个人空间，人际关系，家庭称谓，社交称谓，社区关系，捐款集资等
日常生活	起居作息，上学，工作，打电话，看电视（新闻、天气预报），上网，体育活动，保健，就医，问路，做家务，购物（价格、规格、形状、颜色），生活必需品，外出就餐，饮食习惯等
学校生活	知识，教育，学科，素质教育，学校称谓，学习策略，学校课程，成绩，课堂用语，奖励（奖学金、奖状、表扬），纪律，上学，放学，作业，活动（多元文化活动、课外活动、学校活动、社区活动），学校运动队，假期，家长会，学生会，开学典礼，毕业典礼，师生关系，交朋友，学校设备，图书馆等

话　题	内　容　建　议
家庭生活	婚姻，家庭结构（双亲家庭、单亲家庭），家庭成员，家庭称谓，家长同子女的沟通与理解（代沟），家庭活动，家庭计划，养老，家庭财务管理，家务琐事等
文化娱乐	体育项目，国际比赛，地区比赛，俱乐部活动，游戏，电影，电视，美术，音乐，舞蹈，戏曲，戏剧，体育活动，周末娱乐活动，各种爱好（读书、听音乐、集邮）等
节日活动	节日介绍，各民族的节日，文化节日，个人纪念日，节日的比较等
身心健康	健康（生理、心理），健康意识，运动，食物，饮食习惯，过敏食品，个人卫生，中医西医，健康的生活态度，良好的人际关系，餐桌文化，教育与教养，对健康的认识等
习俗与忌讳	年龄，收入，婚姻状况，健康状况，宗教信仰，政治面貌，带有文化色彩的颜色和数字，不同文化中对隐私的差异和忌讳等
旅游与交通	时间，数字，旅馆，时刻表，问路，看地图，交通标记，交通工具，方向，距离，法制，规定，违法行为等
语言与文化	语言学习策略，语言学习对社会、个人的好处，语言学习的困难，语言和文化的关系，传统思维方式，用多元眼光看事物，了解中国文化并加强对所在国文化的理解等
价值观念	价值观比较，个人与集体，权威与平等，竞争与和谐，美与丑，思想与行动，道德观念等
文学与艺术	审美，意境，意蕴，不同体裁的文学作品（小说、诗歌、散文、报告文学、童话故事等），不同形式的艺术作品（琴、棋、书、画、摄影、雕塑等），不同国家的文学艺术作品欣赏
政治、历史与地理	中国政治结构，中国政策，中国外交，中国法律，中国历史，中国地图，中国江河，中国行政区划，中国邻国等

附录一　汉语教学话题及内容建议表

话　题	内　容　建　议
科学与技术	科学知识，科学普及，技术训练等
全球与环境	全球化，一个地球一个家，保护环境，污染，能源的使用，多种语言教育等
计划与未来	意愿与打算，希望与愿望等
热门话题	全球变暖，自然灾害，难民，污染，毒品，时事政治，上网，战争与和平等
教育	德育，智育，体育，美育，课程，教材，教育体制，教育思想等
植物与动物	花草树木，瓜果梨桃，飞禽走兽等
自然景观	四季，气象（风、云、雷、电），江河湖海，名山大川，日月星辰，世界著名自然景观等

附录二　汉语教学话题及内容举例表

本表是按照本大纲"附录一　汉语教学话题及内容建议表"中的部分内容建议性举例，供使用者参考。教师可根据自己的教学对象进行调整。本附录出现的常用词汇部分收入在"常用汉语800字表"或"常用汉语1500高频词语表"。

个 人 信 息

项　目	任务目标	任务活动（举例）	常用语句	常用词汇
姓名	询问他人的姓名 介绍自己的姓名 介绍他人的姓名	一组人，首先介绍自己的姓名，然后由其中一个人为其他人做介绍。	1. 我叫小明。 2. 我姓王。 3. 我姓李。你呢？ 4. 你叫什么名字？ 5. 您贵姓？	姓，叫，姓名，名字，你，您，我，她，他，你们，我们，他们，中国，日本，美国，去年，
出生地	能正确询问对方的出生地 能正确回答自己的出生地 能正确表达他人的出生地	扮演角色： 一个人说出自己的出生地，另外一个人根据对方的出生地提问别人，并说出自己的出生地。	1. 我在中国出生。 2. 他在美国出生。 3. 你是在日本出生的吗？ 4. 你／您（是）在哪里(国)出生的？	今年，明年，男，女，男孩，女孩，说，语言，英语，日语，法语，德语，阿拉伯语，西班牙语，意大利语，中国人，日本人，韩国人，英国人，澳洲人，美国人，德国人，法国人，加拿大人，意大利人，亚洲，欧洲，
国籍	能正确询问对方的国籍 能说出自己是哪国人 能说出自己会说的语言的名称	老师给学生发一些有不同国家名称的卡片，假定学生的国籍是卡片上的国家，让学生互相询问国籍。	1. 你是哪国人？ 2. 我是中国人。 3. 你是法国人吗？ 4. 不是。我是意大利人。 5. 你会说什么语言？ 6. 我会说英语，也会说法语。	美洲，非洲，做，工作，什么，哪儿，哪个，公司，医院，学校，商店，书店，邮局，银行，小学，

项　目	任务目标	任务活动（举例）	常用语句	常用词汇
职业	能询问职业 能用不同的方式回答问题	学生间相互询问对方或对方的家庭成员做什么工作并回答。	1. 你做什么工作？ 2. 我是老师。 3. 你是老师吧？ 4. 是／不是。 5. 你妈妈在哪儿工作？ 6. 她在银行工作。	中学，大学，学院，老师，职员，学生，警察，售货员，律师，医生，工程师，经理，司机，工人，护士，也

家 人 与 朋 友

项　目	任务目标	任务活动（举例）	常用语句	常用词汇
亲属称谓	能说出常见的亲属称谓	1. 看照片介绍家庭成员； 2. 根据关系描述，说出亲属称谓。	1. 我家有四口人，爸爸、妈妈、哥哥和我。 2. 姐姐比弟弟大三岁。 3. 哥哥是学生，妹妹也是学生。	爸爸，妈妈，哥哥，姐姐，弟弟，妹妹，儿子，女儿，爷爷，奶奶，姥姥（外婆），姥爷（外公），孙子，孙女，外孙子，外孙女，
相互关系	能说明人物之间的关系 能简单评价人物之间的关系	1. 根据情景，描述人物之间的关系； 2. 介绍一个跟自己有关系的人。	1. 我们俩是好朋友。 2. 我们认识10年了。 3. 我们常常一起出国旅游。 4. 我们都喜欢乒乓球，（我们）经常在一起看比赛。	叔叔，妻子，丈夫，男朋友，女朋友，同学，同事，朋友，高，矮，胖，瘦，长，短，大，小，眉毛，眼睛，鼻子，嘴，耳朵，头发，头，

35

项　目	任务目标	任务活动（举例）	常用语句	常用词汇
体貌特征	能简单描述身高、体态 能简单描述衣着 能描述相貌特征	1. 看照片，描述人物的体貌特征； 2. 根据体貌特征，猜人物。	1. 她长得很漂亮。 2. 他长得很帅。 3. 他很高。 4. 他常常穿一件蓝色的大衣。 5. 她长头发，大眼睛，高高的鼻子。 6. 他戴着一副眼镜。	脾气，性格，内向，外向，不爱说话，开朗，随和，急（躁），安静，聪明，勇敢，诚实，可靠，勤奋，认真，努力，能干，灵活，和蔼，骄傲
性格	能说明性格特点 能比较性格差异 能简单评价性格	1. 根据照片，猜测人物的性格特点； 2. 根据情景，描述并评价性格差异。	1. 他比较外向。 2. 她比小王开朗／开朗多了。 3. 他的性格有点儿急。 4. 我的太太比较外向，而我比较内向。	

居 家 生 活

项 目	任务目标	任务活动（举例）	常用语句	常用词汇
居家 环境	能说明房屋的格局	1. 看图，介绍房屋的格局； 2. 看图布置房间； 3. 改变已有的家居布置风格，说明并比较两种方案的特点； 4. 要搬家时，考虑最适合老人的房子具备哪些特点，比如离商店、车站不太远、院子里可以养花等等。	1. 这是我的家。楼上有三间卧室，还有两间浴室。一层有一个大客厅，一个很大的厨房，一个饭厅，和一个厕所。我特别喜欢客厅里的壁炉。书房在地下室，里面有很多书。客房也在地下室。地下室里可以打乒乓球，还可以健身，听音乐。我家虽然不太大，但是很舒适。 2. 这是一套三居室。 3. 这个房间朝阳。 4. 这栋公寓没有电梯。 5. 他的书房里到处都是书。 6. 公寓楼的水电费都很便宜。 7. 房租很贵。	客厅，卧室，书房，厨房，饭厅，厕所，洗手间，娱乐室，客房，车房，门，窗户，窗台，走廊，院子，楼梯，阳台，玻璃，衣柜，书柜，床，书桌，写字台，电视柜，沙发，餐桌，椅子，茶几，橱柜，灯，水龙头，喷头，锁，灶台，水池，窗帘，台布，床单，门帘，电视，音响，音箱，录像机，DVD 机，录音机，VCD 机，洗碗机，热水器，烤箱，冰箱，微波炉，起床，刷牙，洗脸，早饭，午饭，晚饭，上班，下班，锻炼，睡觉，笤帚，拖布，抹布，洗洁精，吸尘器，垃圾桶，垃圾袋，垃圾

项　目	任务目标	任务活动（举例）	常用语句	常用词汇
居家环境			8. 公寓楼和独栋房子相比就显得不大方便，停车比较麻烦。	箱，牙膏，牙刷，毛巾，香皂，洗发水，洗发香波，浴液，好用，前面／边，后面／边，左面／边，右面／边，南面／边，北面／边，东面／边，西面／边，旁边，上面

学习与工作

项　目	任务目标	任务活动（举例）	常用语句	常用词汇
学习生活	能询问别人的学习经历 能正确描述自己的学习经历	1. 用不同的句式互相询问学习汉语的经历，包括学习的时间、地点、内容等； 2. 描述自己的学习经历。	1. 你学了几年汉语了？ 2. 我学了三年汉语了，可是我说得不好。 3. 你学过中国音乐吗？ 4. 我（没）学过中国历史。 5. 汉字很难写。 6. 我已经学会两百多个汉字了。	汉语，英语，法语，德语，日语，韩语，西班牙语，阿拉伯语，写字，唱歌，提问题，复习，温习，工作，实习，打工，进修，住，呆，生活，北京，上海，西门子，海尔，第一，第二，第几，已经，这儿，那儿，

项　目	任务目标	任务活动（举例）	常用语句	常用词汇
工作生活	能询问工作经历 能介绍自己的工作经历	1. 询问别人的工作经历； 2. 介绍自己的工作经历，包括时间、地点、职位、内容等。	1. 我一边上学，一边工作。 2. 她已经工作两年了。 3. 你周末的时候打工吗？ 4. 我现在读高二，周末经常去打工。 5. 你在哪儿工作？ 6. 我在一家公司工作，是一名公司职员。 7. 我在北京工作三个月了。 8. 这是我的名片。	这里，那里，这，那，半，小时，分钟，分，年，月，次，上次，每次，工人，经理，技术员，工程师，职员，经理，名片

爱好与特长

项　目	任务目标	任务活动（举例）	常用语句	常用词汇
爱好	学会问答爱好	1. 采访周围人的兴趣爱好和特长； 2. 列举名人的爱好和特长。	1. 你有什么爱好？ 2. 你喜欢什么运动？ 3. 我爱／喜欢游泳。 4. 我最喜欢购物。 5. 他特别喜欢上网。 6. 我的爸爸喜欢打棒球。 7. 他弟弟特别喜欢踢足球。	游泳，旅游，上网，钓鱼，郊游，探险，骑自行车，爬山，散步，跑步，跳舞，体操，聊天，露营，做饭，健身运动，滑水，滑冰，购物，文学，书法，京剧，舞蹈，戏剧，看小说，电影，电视，戏，打，网球，乒乓球，篮球，排球，足球，羽毛球，板球，游戏，喝茶，听音乐，购物，逛商场
特长	学会问答特长		1. 你有什么特长？ 2. 他网球打得不错。 3. 他做中国菜很拿手。 4. 我不会打网球。	

身 心 健 康

项　目	任务目标	任务活动（举例）	常用语句	常用词汇
看病	能简单地说明自己的病症 能听懂医生的简单问话并回答	1. 老师说出一些常见的症状，请学生说出病名； 2. 老师给出一些常见病名，请学生两人一组扮演医生和病人，互相问答。	1. 你哪儿／哪里不舒服？ 2. 你怎么了？ 3. 我肚子疼得厉害。 4. 请你带我去医院好吗？ 5. 你发烧了，我觉得你应该去看医生。 6. 你脸色不太好，是不是（生）病了？ 7. 你的体温是多少？ 8. 我该去洗牙了。 9. 多休息，多喝水。 10. 嗓子有点儿炎症，吃点消炎药就好了。 11. 我的妈妈刚做了手术，很虚弱。	舒服，不舒服，感冒，生病，头疼，心脏病，肚子痛，癌症，糖尿病，肝炎，艾滋病，洗牙，洗手，医院，诊所，牙科医生，家庭医生，专科医生，手术，护士，急诊，外科，内科，妇科，儿科，老年，中年，青年，少年，幼儿，正常，血压高，血压低，药，开药，化验单，住院，健身，健身房，散步，打太极拳，游泳，爬山，跑步，打网球，跳舞，练瑜伽，健美操，游泳馆，操场，跑步机，广场，运动场，

项　目	任务目标	任务活动（举例）	常用语句	常用词汇
锻炼身体	能询问和说出身体的状况 能说出为了健康而进行的运动	1. 同学间互相询问身体状况； 2. 说说自己锻炼身体的方式。	1. 你每天跑步吗? 2. 我和我的朋友天天慢跑 30 分钟。 3. 早睡早起身体好。 4. 你喜欢运动吗? 5. 你怎么锻炼身体? 6. 我每天早上打太极拳。	中医，看中医，号脉，把脉，针灸，按摩，足疗，望，闻，问，切，中药，药材，中草药，抓药，脉，煎药，药方，汤药，丸药
中医	能听懂医生的指示和诊断内容 借助词典能看懂中药说明书	1. 找两个学生，一个扮演医生，一个扮演病人来看病，练习医生和病人的对话； 2. 到图书馆或上网查到五种中药的名称。	1. 请把舌头伸出来。 2. 先把这三服中药吃完，再来复查。 3. 你的面色发黄。 4. 这种药一天吃几片? 5. 你以前用过针灸吗?	

42

饮　食

项　目	任务目标	任务活动（举例）	常用语句	常用词汇
餐具与厨具	能说出餐具和厨具的名称 能说出中式厨房和本国厨房的基本布置	1. 同学表演用筷子夹豆，看谁夹得快； 2. 出示图片，让学生比较中式厨房和本国厨房的不同。	1. 你会用筷子吗？ 2. 中国人一般不用刀叉吃饭。 3. 请给我一把勺子。 4. 烤箱里的鸡烤好了。 5. 炒菜好吃，但是油烟味儿比较大。	菜单，凉菜，热菜，主食，汤，家常菜，麻婆豆腐，青椒肉丝，北京烤鸭，西红柿鸡蛋汤，吃素，营养素，营养成分，维他命，维生素，矿物质，钙，铁，蛋白质，脂肪，能量，碳水化合物，含有，不能吃……（过敏），中餐，西餐，点心，日本料理，意大利菜，法国菜，风味，小吃，酸，甜，苦，辣，咸，油腻，清淡，好吃，生，熟，热，凉，
食品与饮料	能谈论和询问喜欢和不喜欢的食物 能询问和谈论日常饮食	1. 列一张购物单，写出你需要在菜市场买的食品，然后与同伴比较； 2. 请学生列举本国人最难接受的和最喜欢的中国食品，并简单说明理由。教师可提供一些帮助。	1. 你喜欢吃什么？ 2. 你吃米饭还是面条？ 3. 你吃过饺子吗？ 4. 我不爱喝咖啡。 5. 我吃了面包、小肉肠，还喝了杯牛奶。 6. 你们想喝什么饮料？ 7. 绿茶有益于身体健康。	

43

项　目	任务目标	任务活动（举例）	常用语句	常用词汇
外出就餐	会看菜单点菜 会询问所点菜的情况 会评价食物和饮料的味道	1. 准备中文菜单（凉菜、热菜、主食的名称及价钱等），表演在饭馆吃饭：点菜、结账等； 2. 假设自己是饭馆老板，为自家饭馆做一个广告。	1. 我们看一下儿菜单。 2. 今天有什么特别推荐的菜，请你介绍一下儿。 3. 想吃点儿什么？ 4. 我喜欢海鲜。 5. 我想点一道法国菜。 6. 中国的火锅很有特色。 7. 这个菜是用什么做的？ 8. 结账（买单）！	点菜，结账，买单，打包，饿，饱，渴，服务员，小姐，服务生，烹调，炒，煎，烧，煮，炖，烤，蒸，筷子，盘子，刀，叉，锅，碗，杯子，汤匙，勺，烤肉，牛排，小羊排，炖牛肉，香肠，沙拉，番茄酱，盐，胡椒，饮料，汽水，可乐，果汁，咖啡，茶，雪碧
饮食习惯	了解基本的烹调方法 能谈论和询问个人的饮食习惯 能谈论和询问本国和其他国家的饮食习惯	1. 按照中文菜谱实际做一个中国菜，大家品尝后对味道作出评价； 2. 扮成记者，采访班上同学的饮食习惯，如："你能吃辣的吗？"，然后报告出来。	1. 日本菜有什么特点？ 2. 日本人常吃生的菜。 3. 中国菜有点儿油腻。 4. 今天我们准备了烤肉和沙拉。 5. 我喜欢清淡点儿的菜。 6. 我不吃辣的。 7. 我们常吃鱼。 8. 太咸了！	

问 价 与 购 物

项　目	任务目标	任务活动（举例）	常用语句	常用词汇
货币	能说出常见货币的名称 认识人民币 学会说钱数	1. 看图片，说出人民币的面值； 2. 看价签，说出钱数。	25.80元——二十五块／元八毛 102.38元——一百零二元三角八分	人民币，美元，欧元，日元，英镑，元（块），角（毛），分，公斤，斤，两，磅，千克，水果，苹果，梨，香蕉，西瓜，草莓，桔子，葡萄，桃，服装，上衣，裤子，西装，裙子，衬衫，T恤，鞋，帽子，袜子，件，条，双，套，个，张，台，罐，包，瓶，盒，大号，中号，小号，米，公分，尺，寸，大，小，长，短，肥，瘦，便宜，贵，打折，多少，钱，零钱，信用卡，收银台，收据，红，绿，蓝，黄，黑，白，灰，
单位与尺码	能说出常见商品名称及量词 了解商品型号或尺码	1. 列出常见的商品名称； 2. 列出购物清单。	一条裙子 两双袜子 一斤苹果 一袋米	
价格	能说明需求 学会问答商品的价格 学会还价的简单说法 学会付款的常用语句	1. 看价签，问答商品的价格； 2. 根据卡片提示，进行角色扮演，顾客和小贩买东西。（包括：提出需求、问价钱、讨价还价、付款）	1. 我要一杯咖啡。 2. 我买一本书。 3. 可以试试吗？ 4. 这个多少钱？ 5. 苹果多少钱一斤？ 6. 这个有点儿贵，能便宜点儿吗？ 7. 可以打折吗？ 8. 我买两个，能便宜点儿吗？ 9. 给您钱。 10. 找您五块钱。 11. 能用信用卡吗？	

项　目	任务目标	任务活动（举例）	常用语句	常用词汇
性状与质量	学会说明颜色 学会说明材质 学会简单地评价商品	1. 看商品图片，说明颜色、材质、并简单评价商品； 2. 列出家里或教室里物品的名称、颜色、材质、质量等。	1. 我要买一辆红色的车。 2. 这件衬衫是纯棉的。 3. 太贵了。 4. 太长了。 5. 挺时髦的。	棕，金色，深（蓝等），纯，棉，毛，丝，麻，玻璃，金，银，木，好，坏，真，假，退，换
退货换货	学会提出要求 学会说明原因	根据卡片上提示的原因和理由，提出退换货要求。（如：颜色不合适、质量不好、大小不合适等）。	1. 这个能退吗？ 2. 可以换一个吗？ 3. 这种颜色不适合我。	

银　行

项　目	任务目标	任务活动（举例）	常用语句	常用词汇
开户	能顺利在银行开户	1. 填写一张开户单； 2. 两人对话完成开户的任务。	1. 我要开一个账户。 2. 请把这张单子填一下儿。 3. 活期的还是定期的？ 4. 我要兑换一点儿外汇。	储蓄，付款，支票，汇款，存折，定期，活期，股票，退休金，账号，账户，户头，填表，手续费，储蓄卡，身份证，美元，英镑，欧元，日元，人民币，零钱，整钱，纸币，硬币，面额，面值，兑换，

46

项　目	任务目标	任务活动（举例）	常用语句	常用词汇
存钱 取钱	能清楚地说明自己的目的：存多少钱，取多少钱	1. 按要求填写一张人民币存款单； 2. 填写一张取款单，并分角色表演。	1. 我要存2000元人民币。 2. 我想取1000美元。 3. 自动取款机在哪儿？ 4. 请输入密码。 5. 我可以直接取美元吗？ 6. 我不会填写取款单。	汇率，收据，投资
换钱	能正确地说明自己换多少钱（外币换人民币） 能说清楚自己换多少零钱	1. 每位同学轮流扮演兑换处的工作人员，让其余同学分别用自己国家的货币去兑换人民币（适合国际班）； 2. 请两个学生分角色表演，将100元人民币换成一张50元的，两张20元的和两张5元的。	1. 您要换多少？ 2. 我想换1000欧元。 3. 换成人民币。 4. 我想把这张纸币换成硬币。 5. 今天的汇率是多少？ 6. 请拿好。 7. 我想把美元换成人民币。 8. 请把这张单子填好。	

旅 游 与 交 通

项 目	任务目标	任务活动（举例）	常用语句	常用词汇
问路	会问路，并能听懂所指的方向 会给问路者指明方向	1. 说出一个地方，学生需问路才能找到，先到者为胜； 2. 两种表示店铺和建筑的地图（A 和 B），持有 B 地图的人向持有 A 地图的人询问要去的地方（只在 A 地图上）的路线，持有 A 地图的人指路，然后互换角色。	1. 请问，去北京大学怎么走？ 2. 附近有没有银行？ 3. 往前走，到红绿灯向右拐。 4. 要走多长时间？ 5. 往前走 100 米就到了。 6. 得坐车吗？ 7. 还是打车去吧。 8. 过了马路就到了。	走，坐车，往，拐，转，米，公尺，公里，对面，旁边，附近，红绿灯，路口，十字路口，远，近，楼上，楼下，前，后，左，右，东，西，南，北，交通工具，公共汽车，巴士，地铁，轮船，火车，飞机，汽车，自行车，出租车，长途车，走路，换（倒）车，买票，上，下，座位，售票员，查票员，软卧，硬卧，硬座，检票，订票，经济舱，航班，航空公司，转机，单程，往返，登机，行李，托运，安检，机场班车，车站，机场，售票处，站台，车厢，登机口，候车（机）室，列车员，司机，
交通工具	会乘坐公共汽车、地铁、出租车等公共交通工具 会乘坐火车、飞机等交通工具	1. 角色扮演：学生扮成售票员和乘客，说出乘车时最常用的交际语句； 2. 将学生分成正方与反方两组进行辩论，以"骑自行车好还是开车好？"为题，分别陈述理由，说明这两种主要交通工具的利与弊。	1. 到故宫坐几路车？ 2. 在哪儿倒／换车？ 3. 一张颐和园。 4. 这个位子有没有人坐？ 5. 下车。 6. 劳驾。 7. 飞机就要起飞（降落）了。 8. 去人民大会堂。	

项　目	任务目标	任务活动（举例）	常用语句	常用词汇
预订	会预订机票、车票等 会预订旅馆房间	1. 认读航班，打电话预订机票； 2. 打电话预订房间，并询问有关房间的简单情况（是否安静、能否吸烟、有什么设备等）。	1. 我要预订一张去上海的机票。 2. 有今天下午去西安的经济舱吗？多少钱？ 3. 我要预订一个双人间，住两晚。 4. 带洗澡间吗？含早餐吗？	乘客，空姐，出发，到达，起飞，正点，准点，晚点，预订，安排，旅馆，房间，单人间，双人间，房间号，钥匙，洗澡间，卫生间，厕所，餐厅，前台，服务，打扫，叫醒，送餐，洗衣，请勿打扰，手续，入住，退房，结账，现金，信用卡，旅行支票，免税，个人物品，报关，护照，入境，出境，海关，检查，（填写）申报单，登记卡，签证，护照，国籍
办理 手续	会办理酒店入住及退房手续 会办理出入境手续	1. 学生两人一组分别扮演在饭店前台办理入住及退房手续； 2. 模拟海关出入境场景，请学生演习。	1. 请填一下儿海关申报单（入境登记卡）。 2. 请出示您的护照。 3. 请把包里的东西都拿出来。 4. 我已经预订了一个双人间。 5. 这张画不能带出境。 6. 有空房间吗？ 7. 请填一下儿住宿登记卡。 8. 我要退房了，请结账。	

项　目	任务目标	任务活动（举例）	常用语句	常用词汇
酒店服务	会提出一些服务要求	1. 角色扮演，入住旅馆后要求某些客房服务（送餐、叫醒服务、洗衣等）； 2. 因对酒店服务不满，找相关人员投诉。	1. 请明早6点叫醒我。 2. 我需要客房服务。 3. 我房间的空调坏了。 4. 请把这个包拿到808房间。	

态 度 与 情 感

项　目	任务目标	任务活动（举例）	常用语句	常用词汇
喜欢	能表达喜欢的情感	教师准备一些笑脸图片和一些活动图片，请学生分别抽签。然后叙述两张图片的内容。一个笑脸，说明自己喜欢抽到的活动，两个笑脸说明自己非常喜欢抽到的活动，三个笑脸则说明自己特别喜欢。鼓励学生使用不同的句式。	1. 你喜欢这本书吗？ 2. 我非常喜欢这本书。 3. 我对跳舞非常感兴趣。 4. 她特别爱听京剧。 5. 你喜欢不喜欢这本书？ 6. 我特别喜欢二胡。	很，非常，太，特别，喜欢，爱，兴趣，怎么样，好吗，行吗，好，行，好的，可以，同意，没问题，对不起，抱歉，想，要，能，可以，觉得，认为，但是，可是，建议，意见，看法，想法，打算，说好，办法，同意，不同意，反对，不行，不可以，不可能

项　目	任务目标	任务活动（举例）	常用语句	常用词汇
不喜欢	能表达不喜欢的情感	游戏： 教师准备一些活动卡片，展示给学生后反扣在黑板上，将学生分两组。各选取一名学生上台，每组分别说自己不喜欢卡片上的某活动，注意尽量不用重复的句子。台上的同学根据记忆找出该活动的图片，找对了得分，找错了不得分。得分高的组胜出。	1. 我不爱看电影。 2. 我对电视不感兴趣。 3. 你觉得这部电影怎么样？ 4. 我不太喜欢喝茶。 5. 我不喜欢暴力电影。 6. 我不喜欢跑步，但我喜欢打球。 7. 我不喜欢小狗，我喜欢大狗。 8. 我不喜欢打听别人的私事，也不爱听。 9. 我不喜欢骂人。	
同意	能用合适的方式表达同意的态度	游戏： 老师准备一些说法，由学生来快速判断，如果说法正常（如："现在我们说汉语吧"），学生则选择表示同意的语句回答，如果说法不正常（如："到夜里十二点了。"），学生则说，不。判断出错者出局，坚持到最后者胜出。	1. 我没有意见。 2. 我同意你的看法。 3. 你的建议不错。 4. 你说的一点儿都不错。 5. 我也是这么想的。 6. 我们一起去书店怎么样？ 7. 好／好的。 8. 我们去听中国文化讲座，好不好？ 9. 我答应李伟明天下午一起去看电影。	

51

项 目	任务目标	任务活动（举例）	常用语句	常用词汇
不同意	能用合适的方式表达不同意的态度	辩论比赛：学生分成两组，按照卡片提示一组说明一种观点，另一组用不同的方式表示不同意见。	1. 我不同意你的意见。 2. 这种说法不对。 3. 他的说法太可笑了。 4. 这种说法有问题。 5. 这种观点不正确。 6. 你的意见我同意是同意，不过还有些问题需要考虑。	

计 划

项 目	任务目标	任务活动（举例）	常用语句	常用词汇
计划	学会问答时间、日期 学会问答计划	1. 看钟表说时间； 2. 看日历说日期； 3. 列出亲朋好友的生日； 4. 制订假期计划； 5. 日常生活安排。	1. 现在几点了？ 2. 现在两点半。 3. 你的生日是几月几号？ 4. 我的生日是 6 月 8 号。 5. 今天星期几？ 6. 今天星期三。 7. 这个周末你打算／准备做什么？ 8. 我想／要／打算去天安门。 9. 几点了？	点，分（钟），秒，半，一刻，差，年，月，日，星期，礼拜，打算，计划，准备，要，想，周末，夏天，暑假，春天，寒假，圣诞节，感恩节，宗教节日，新年，春节，中秋节，端午节，黄金周，长假

社 会 交 往

项　目	任务目标	任务活动（举例）	常用语句	常用词汇
请求	学会提出请求 学会委婉地提出请求	1. 请求别人做一件事； 2. 模拟求婚。	1. 劳驾，请把那本词典递给我。 2. 把奶油递给我好吗？谢谢。 3. 拜托了。 4. 你能帮我个忙吗？ 5. 你愿意跟我结婚吗？ 6. 你愿意做我的女朋友吗？	劳驾，请，求，可以，建议，怎么样，帮忙，帮助
建议	学会征求建议 学会提出建议 学会委婉地提出建议	1. 根据不同情景征求或提出建议； 2. 根据不同情景委婉地提出建议。	1. 我的建议如何？ 2. 你有什么建议？ 3. 我希望我们周末能一起去游泳。 4. 周末我们去长城，好吗？	

天　气

项　目	任务目标	任务活动（举例）	常用语句	常用词汇
季节	能说出中国和自己国家季节的名称 能简单描述不同季节的特点	1. 准备四个季节的风景图片，让学生说说各是什么季节和主要景物； 2. 小组练习：两个同学一组，互相说一说自己的城市一年中的气候变化。每个同学记住对方的城市气候的特点，然后向全班同学报告。	1. 一年有几个季节？ 2. 你最喜欢什么季节？ 3. 这里春天很温暖，夏天很炎热，秋天很凉快，冬天很寒冷。 4. 北京的春天怎么样？ 5. 北京一年四季分明。 6. 这里冬季寒冷干燥，夏季高温多雨。 7. 哈尔滨冬天的最低气温能达到零下 40°C。 8. 北京的秋天最好。 9. 我最怕热！	雾，阳光，风，雷，闪电，雷阵雨，潮湿，干燥，暖和，热，桑拿天，凉快，冷，降温，晴朗，阴天，多云，晴转阴，晴转多云，大风，刮风，（下）雨，（下）雪，季节，气候，四季，春天，夏天，秋天，冬天，旱季，雨季，很，非常，特别，极了，够，挺，最，温度，气温，升高，降低，保暖，防寒，摄氏度，天气预报，播送，地区，零下，白天，夜间，四季分明，大风降温

项 目	任务目标	任务活动（举例）	常用语句	常用词汇
气候特点	能简单说出关于气候的表述（冷、热、凉、暖等） 能听懂最基本的关于天气的用语 能说出气候的地区差异	1. 准备一些表现天气情况的图片，让学生说一说各是什么天气； 2. 给学生准备地图，请学生根据听到的天气预报，在地图上标出各城市的天气情况，并向全班报告； 3. 比较自己所在城市与中国哈尔滨、北京和广州的气候差异。	1. 明天天气怎么样？ 2. 今天天气真好。 3. 今天可能会下雨，出门要带雨伞。 4. 今天真够热的。 5. 秋天到了，天气越来越凉了。 6. 今天的最高气温只有 5°C。 7. 今天的气温比昨天高 3°C。 8. 海南比北京热多了。 9. 上海冬天没有北京冷。 10. 今天有五级风。 11. 雪越下越大。 12. 南方和北方温差很大。 13. 家家户户都关心全球气候的变暖。	

55

自　然

项　目	任务目标	任务活动（举例）	常用语句	常用词汇
植物	能说出常见植物的名称 能简单说出植物的特点 能简单介绍植物的功能	1. 看植物的图片，认读植物的名称； 2. 说出三种常见植物的特点及功能，并作出简单的评价。	1. 这朵花真香。 2. 迎春花在春天开。 3. 竹子的中间是空的。 4. 牡丹花真漂亮。 5. 今年葡萄长得很好。 6. 植树造林对保护环境有好处。 7. 很多植物都可以作为药材。	树，草，森林，绿化，松树，杨树，柳树，竹子，苹果树，柿子树，枣树，花，玫瑰，牡丹，菊花，兰花，梅花，勿忘我，迎春花，康乃馨，野花，粮食，小麦，大米，白薯，花生，玉米，大豆，土豆，马铃薯，燕麦，种，种植，种地，养，植物，药材，狗，猫，牛，马，羊，鸡，猪，鸭子，鸟，猴子，老虎，兔子，蛇，狮子，大象，熊猫，肉食动物，食草动物，宇宙，银河系，太阳系，太阳，水星，金星，木星，火星，土星，天王星，海王星，冥王星，地球，月亮，公转，自转，大爆炸，黑洞，彗星，行星，恒星，卫星，地震，海啸，
动物	能说出常见动物的名称 能简单介绍常见动物的习性	1. 列出中国的十二生肖； 2. 介绍一种你最喜欢的动物。	1. 熊猫喜欢吃竹叶。 2. 狗会看家。 3. 除了熊猫，别的动物我都不太喜欢。 4. 金鱼不好养。 5. 我养的小鸟很可爱。	
天体知识	能说出重要天体的名称 能简单了解天体的基本知识	1. 看图说出天体的名称； 2. 介绍自己了解的天体知识； 3. 上网阅读中文有关自然灾害的信息。	1. 月亮是地球的卫星。 2. 太阳是一颗恒星。 3. 月亮本身不发光。	

56

项　目	任务目标	任务活动（举例）	常用语句	常用词汇
自然灾害	能说出自然灾害的名称	1. 看图片，说出自然灾害的名称； 2. 看图片，说明自然灾害的成因和结果以及预防措施。	1. 这次地震的震中在太平洋海底。 2. 这次海啸是由地震引起的。 3. 这次水灾造成3000多人死亡。 4. 除了人员伤亡外，这次火灾还造成了巨大的财产损失。	火山，喷发，洪水，飓风，冰雹，水灾，火灾，旱灾，虫灾，难民，灭火器

语言学习

项　目	任务目标	任务活动（举例）	常用语句	常用词汇
语言学习中的困难	在遇到问题时知道如何提问 能够表述汉语学习中的困难，并说明理由	1. 说一说自己在学习汉语中遇到的困难； 2. 说一说自己在学习汉语中遇到困难时的一些解决办法。	1. 这个字／词用汉语怎么说？ 2. 我的发音不太好。 3. 声调不对。 4. 汉语发音不太难。 5. 汉字很难写，可是非常有意思。 6. 请你再说一遍。 7. 请你说慢／清楚一点儿。	拼音，读音，声调，声母，韵母，元音，辅音，儿化，四声，发音，汉字，偏旁，部首，笔画，笔顺，多音字，简体字，繁体字，词类，名词，动词，形容词，副词，连词，助词，叹词，介词，汉语，方言，书面语，外来语，

项 目	任务目标	任务活动（举例）	常用语句	常用词汇
语言学习策略	能听懂别人介绍的学习方法 能说出自己的学习方法	1. 教师在黑板上写出一些普遍的学习策略，请大家选出跟自己相同的策略； 2. 学生两人一组，交流自己的学习习惯。	1. 上课之前先预习。 2. 大声朗读生词／课文。 3. 每天课后要复习。 4. 经常看生词表。 5. 经常和中国人聊天。 6. 每天早上听15分钟的汉语录音。 7. 每天读一篇汉语文章。 8. 制订一个学习计划表。 9. 认真完成作业。	术语, 例句, 搭配, 复习, 聊天, 听录音, 看生词, 读, 提问, 上网, 学习, 作业, 抄写, 毛笔字, 朗读, 清晰, 清楚, 准确
汉字	能识别和辨认常见的汉字偏旁或部首	1. 把全班同学分为两组，教师给每个组相同的20个常用汉字的形旁和声旁，给每组两分钟的时间准备，让他们利用这些偏旁拼出汉字来，并写出汉字的读音；	1. 这个字是多音字。 2. 这个字怎么读? 3. 这个汉字的笔画很多。 4. 这是个左右结构的汉字。 5. 这个偏旁的意思是水。 6. 我们没学过这个字。	

项　目	任务目标	任务活动（举例）	常用语句	常用词汇
汉字		2. 教师把一则小故事抄写在黑板上，其中有许多字是笔画不全的，要求学生逐一指出并补正。	7. 汉字太有趣了！ 8. 他很聪明，汉字一学就会了。	

文 学 艺 术

项　目	任务目标	任务活动（举例）	常用语句	常用词汇
文学艺术	能简要说明文学作品的形式 能简要说明其他艺术形式	1. 请简单介绍自己知道的文学艺术作品的内容； 2. 看艺术图片，说出作品、作者及主要的艺术形象。	1. 你喜欢中国诗词吗？ 2. 你看过《西游记》吗？ 3. 诗歌是中国唐朝的主要文学形式。 4. 明清时期中国小说很繁荣。 5. 他书架上的书不是中国古典小说就是外国名著。	诗歌，散文，小说，雕塑，摄影，绘画，戏剧，周（朝），唐（朝），宋（朝），元（朝），明（朝），清（朝），《诗经》，《红楼梦》，《三国演义》，《水浒传》，《西游记》，《狂人日记》，《家》，李白，杜甫，陆游，曹雪芹，罗贯中，

项 目	任务目标	任务活动（举例）	常用语句	常用词汇
名家名作	简要了解著名作家及其作品 简要了解著名艺术家及其作品		1. 你能介绍一下儿唐朝诗人李白的情况吗？ 2.《西游记》是一部有名的中国古典小说。 3. 只要提起唐朝诗人，人们就会想到李白。 4. 只有杜甫才称得上是"诗圣"。	施耐庵，吴承恩，鲁迅，巴金，老舍，丁西林，孙悟空，唐僧，诸葛亮，刘备，曹操，宋江，林冲，贾宝玉，林黛玉
经典艺术形象	简要了解文学艺术中的经典艺术形象 简要了解其他艺术中的经典艺术形象		1. 林黛玉是哪部小说中的人物？ 2. 阿Q是一个什么样的人物？ 3. 在中国，不管大人还是小孩儿，都知道孙悟空。	

历 史 地 理

项 目	任务目标	任务活动（举例）	常用语句	常用词汇
历史人物	能说出中国历史上一些比较有名的人物，并对其事迹有大致的了解	给出一些历史名人的照片，并将其名字写在小卡片发给学生，让学生在相应的照片下贴上名字。	1. 你知道毛泽东吗？ 2. 秦始皇是中国历史上的第一位皇帝。 3. 孔子是中国伟大的思想家。	历史，朝代，公元，公元前，中世纪，孔子，秦始皇，李白，成吉思汗，毛泽东，郑和，丝绸之路，

项　目	任务目标	任务活动（举例）	常用语句	常用词汇
历史 人物			4. 孔子不但是伟大的思想家，而且还是伟大的教育家。	新中国成立，世界，亚洲，欧洲，非洲，美洲，大洋洲，国家，首都，人口，省，市，自治区，直辖市，特别行政区，县，
历史 事件	能说出中国历史上一些比较有名的历史事件 能说出自己国家历史上比较有名的历史事件	历史图片展：每个人给自己喜欢的一张历史图片（如：历史上的名人、古迹、事件等）配上简短的介绍，制成一张图文并茂的展品，先向大家展示和口头介绍，然后把它贴在教室的墙上。	1. 丝绸之路是从西安开始的。 2. 你听说过"郑和下西洋"的故事吗？ 3. 你知道中华人民共和国是什么时候成立的吗？ 4. 历史与其说是伟人创造的，还不如说是人民创造的。 5. 屈原宁可投江自尽，也不愿苟且偷生。	州，省会，首府，平原，高原，山地，盆地，草原，森林，沙漠，海湾，河流，湖，江，林业，农业，工业，旅游业，商业，铁矿，煤矿，石油，木材，出产，进出口，制造，电子产品，生产

61

项 目	任务目标	任务活动（举例）	常用语句	常用词汇
地理常识	能在地图上指出中国的位置并说出中国的首都和各省的省会 能知道中国主要相邻的国家的名称 能说出自己国家的名称、首都及各州／省的名称和主要城市 能说出中国的人口情况 能说出本国的产业概况	两人一组，手拿一张中国地图，一人说出一个省的名字，另一人快速查找，并说出在中国的地理位置。各说 10 个，比比看，谁找得又快又准。	1. 中国的首都是北京。 2. 我家在美国的华盛顿州。 3. 中国有 13.6 亿人，是世界上人口最多的国家。 4. 中国的西部有高原。 5. 中国是一个地大物博、人口众多的国家。	

宗教民俗

项 目	任务目标	任务活动（举例）	常用语句	常用词汇
宗教	对中国的主要宗教有所了解 对世界主要宗教有所了解	老师展示不同宗教的图片（教堂、寺庙、清真寺、宗教人物图片），学生加以说明。	1. 这是北京最大的清真寺。 2. 我们一家人都信天主教。 3. 佛教大约是在公元 1 世纪时传到中国来的。	佛教，基督教，天主教，伊斯兰教，印度教，宗教，教堂，牧师，神父，礼拜，聚会，祈祷，圣诞节，复活节，斋戒，朝圣，佛堂，

项　目	任务目标	任务活动（举例）	常用语句	常用词汇
宗教	能表达自己的宗教信仰，叙述自己经常进行的宗教活动			烧香，寺庙，皈依，吃斋，念佛
民俗与文化	对中国的一些民俗文化、成语故事以及现在活跃在世界各地的杰出华人有所了解	老师讲一个中国神话故事或民间传说，然后让学生复述。	1. 龙是中华民族的象征。 2. 旗袍不仅是中国的，也是世界的。 3. 中国民间有一个传统习俗，过春节的时候，全家团圆，一起吃年夜饭。 4. 红色在中国传统文化中表示大吉大利。	

附录三 中国文化题材及文化任务举例表

本表仅为使用者提供一些相应的题材内容，使用者可以参照题材内容自行发挥，其中大部分题材可以通用，也可以根据需要在不同等级中重复使用。

一级文化题材及文化任务举例

题 材	学 习 任 务	跨文化交际思考问题举例
风俗礼仪	1. 初步了解中国人见面时的礼节：除"你好"外，也用"您好"、"吃饭了吗？"或者"去哪儿？"等表示问候； 2. 初步了解中国人赋予颜色的文化含义：如红色表示喜庆； 3. 初步了解中国人赋予数字的文化含义：喜欢数字6表示顺利；8谐音"发"；9表示长久；不喜欢数字4，谐音"死"。	1) 所在国的人们见面时的礼节是什么？跟中国人有什么不同？ 2) 所在国用什么颜色表示喜庆？红色有什么特殊的涵义吗？ 3) 所在国对数字有没有什么禁忌？人们喜欢什么数字，为什么？不喜欢什么数字，为什么？
家庭称谓	1. 了解并熟悉中国人姓名的表述：姓在前、名在后；姓名后加"老师"、"先生"、"女士"、"太太"等。此外，中国人的姓、名有时是单字，有时是由两个字组成的； 2. 初步了解中国人的家族观念：重视家庭关系；中国人家人之间的称谓：爸爸、妈妈、哥哥、姐姐、弟弟、妹妹，以及孩子一般不当面称呼父母姓名的习俗。	1) 所在国的姓名表述方式跟中国一样吗？如果不一样，请说说有什么不同。 2) 在所在国，孩子可以当面称呼父母姓名吗？家人之间怎么相互称呼？

题　材	学　习　任　务	跨文化交际思考问题举例
生肖 属相	1. 了解十二生肖的名称及顺序：鼠、牛、虎、兔、龙、蛇、马、羊、猴、鸡、狗、猪以及它们与公历年之间的相互对应关系；熟悉自己的属相； 2. 了解中国关于属相的传说：鼠为什么排在第一位？	1) 所在国有没有类似十二生肖的年龄计数方式？ 2) 它跟十二生肖有没有相同或不同的地方？ 3) 所在国有没有十二星座？如果有，请说说它和生肖的不同。 4) 所在国有没有类似的传说？

二级文化题材及文化任务举例

题　材	学　习　任　务	跨文化交际思考问题举例
音乐 舞蹈 绘画	1. 了解中国独特的音乐以及它的简单分类：古典音乐、民族音乐、流行音乐等；知道最常见的中国传统乐器的名称，如古筝、二胡等； 2. 简单了解中国的民族舞蹈； 3. 了解中国拥有丰富而独特的绘画艺术，认识一般的中国山水画。	1) 中国的传统音乐跟所在国的传统音乐一样吗？中国的流行音乐与所在国的流行音乐有什么相似之处？ 2) 所在国的民族舞蹈跟中国的民族舞蹈有什么相似之处吗？ 3) 所在国独特的绘画艺术形式是什么？
体育	1. 了解太极拳是中国最著名的武术形式之一；能辨别太极拳与其他武术形式； 2. 了解中国比较普及的大众体育运动：乒乓球、羽毛球、游泳、跑步等。	1) 你能说说太极拳跟所在国比较流行的健身方式的不同吗？ 2) 所在国比较普及的大众体育运动是什么？
交通	1. 熟悉中国的日常交通工具：自行车、汽车、公共汽车、无轨电车、地铁、出租车、火车、飞机等； 2. 理解自行车在中国交通中的重要地位，了解中国汽车越来越多的现状以及汽车越来越多所带来的问题。	1) 说说所在国日常的交通工具有哪些？ 2) 所在国最重要的交通工具是什么？自行车在所在国交通中处于什么地位？

题 材	学 习 任 务	跨文化交际思考问题举例
大众传媒	1. 了解广播、电视、报刊、杂志等大众传媒形式； 2. 说出所在国权威的报刊杂志、电台和电视台的名称。	1) 你能说出所在国有影响的电视台、电视频道和电台吗？ 2) 你最爱看哪个频道的节目？为什么？

三级文化题材及文化任务举例

题 材	学 习 任 务	跨文化交际思考问题举例
地理	1. 熟悉中国主要邻国的名称：俄罗斯、韩国、越南、日本、印度等； 2. 了解中国主要邻国与中国的地理位置关系。	所在国的邻国都有哪些？请说出他们的中文名称。
建筑	简单了解中国传统建筑的名称及其基本特点，如：四合院、平房等。	对比所在国和中国的房屋建筑的不同。
教育	1. 初步了解中国学校的设置：幼儿园、小学、初中、高中、中专、大学、成人教育； 2. 了解并熟悉中国学校的课程设置：必修课、选修课；主课、副课的名称等。	1) 所在国学校的设置跟中国一样吗？ 2) 每一个阶段各是几年？ 3) 所在国学校的课程设置跟一般中国学校的课程设置有没有不同之处？如果有，请指出。
风俗礼仪	1. 了解中国人送礼物和接受礼物的习惯表达方式，如：不当面打开礼物等； 2. 了解中国人过生日的传统习俗：吃长寿面以及现代中国多数人喜欢吃蛋糕的变化； 3. 初步了解中国人告别时的礼节：除"再见"外，还有"留步"、"慢走"等表达方式以及与此相关的送客人一程的告别习惯。	1) 所在国送礼物和接受礼物的习惯表达方式有哪些？ 2) 所在国接受礼物时能不能当面打开？ 3) 所在国过生日的时候有什么传统习俗？ 4) 所在国在告别时主人和客人会不会说类似于"慢走"和"留步"的话？为什么？

题　材	学　习　任　务	跨文化交际思考问题举例
音乐 舞蹈 绘画	1. 了解并欣赏一些著名的中国古典音乐和民族音乐； 2. 了解并欣赏一些著名的中国民族舞蹈； 3. 了解一些中国历史上著名的画家并欣赏其作品等。	1) 你能列举出一些所在国古典音乐、民族音乐和经典流行音乐作品的名称吗？ 2) 所在国有什么民族舞蹈？ 3) 所在国比较有名的画家有哪些？他们的代表作是什么？你觉得它们跟中国画有什么异同？

四级文化题材及文化任务举例

题　材	学　习　任　务	跨文化交际思考问题举例
地理	1. 了解中国的地形特征：地形复杂；山区面积广； 2. 了解中国的地势特征：西高东低； 3. 了解中国著名的山川河流的名称，如：长江、黄河、泰山等。	1) 对比中国地形与所在国及所在大洲的地形的不同，说出所在国地形的特点。 2) 你知道所在国或所在大洲的地势特点吗？它们跟中国的地势特点一样吗？
戏剧	1. 了解中国戏剧的种类，比较流行的剧种有京剧、越剧、黄梅戏等。其中，京剧是中国的国剧； 2. 了解中国戏剧的几个常见曲目名称及简单故事梗概，如《西厢记》等。	1) 你能说出中国戏剧跟你们所在国戏剧之间的一些相同点吗？ 2) 所在国的戏剧有没有类似脸谱的化妆方法？ 3) 所在国有没有类似《宝莲灯》的戏剧故事？
节日	简单了解中国关于春节、端午节、中秋节的传说；"年"兽的故事；屈原的传说；嫦娥奔月等。	1) 请举出所在国最重要的一些节日，并说出它们的来源。 2) 你认为所在国哪个节日的重要性类似于中国的春节？为什么？

题　材	学　习　任　务	跨文化交际思考问题举例
交通	1. 能看懂中国的公共汽车站牌； 2. 了解中国火车车次的表述方式，如：Z表示直达车；Y表示旅游车；T表示特快车；K表示快车等。	1) 所在国的公共汽车站牌站名排列方式跟中国有什么不同？你觉得哪个更方便？为什么？ 2) 所在国的飞机航班表述方式是什么？你能描述一下吗？
风俗	1. 了解春节是中国最重要的传统节日及其风俗习惯：吃年夜饭、贴春联、拜年、吃饺子等； 2. 了解端午节是中国民间比较重要的节日及其风俗习惯：赛龙舟、吃粽子、插艾条等； 3. 了解中秋节是中国的团圆节及其风俗习惯：吃月饼、赏月。	1) 中国的春节有倒贴福字的习惯，取谐音义：福到了。所在国传统节日中有没有类似的利用谐音求吉利的做法？ 2) 所在国的团圆节是哪个？有哪些风俗习惯？
音乐舞蹈绘画	1. 进一步了解中国音乐并学习一些简单的民歌和流行歌曲； 2. 了解一些常见的民族乐器并能识别它们的乐声； 3. 了解中国现代比较流行的舞蹈形式； 4. 了解中国画的一些艺术特征，如：留白、大写意等。	1) 结合所在国的音乐，说说你对中国音乐的理解。 2) 所在国跟中国有没有共同流行的舞蹈形式？ 3) 结合所在国的绘画特征，说说你对中国画的理解。
体育	1. 了解目前中国和所在国的各项体育运动在世界体坛的地位； 2. 知道刘翔、姚明等国际体育明星。	1) 所在国在世界体坛水平比较高的运动项目是什么？ 2) 说出一些所在国的国际体育明星。
大众传媒	1. 了解中国网络常用的域名特征：.cn等； 2. 尝试使用汉语网络查找自己所需的资料。	列出几个所在国网络常用域名的后缀，如：.edu、.com等。

68

五级文化题材及文化任务举例

题　材	学 习 任 务	跨文化交际思考问题举例
气候地理	1. 了解中国气候的多样性及其主要特征：冬冷夏热、冬干夏雨； 2. 了解中国的行政区划：分为34个省级行政单位，下设地区、县等； 3. 了解主要的省会城市，如：北京、上海、广州、天津等； 4. 知道主要大城市的名字及其在中国的地理位置。	1) 对比所在国跟中国的气候特征有哪些不同。 2) 说说所在国跟中国行政区划的不同之处。 3) 所在国有没有城市跟中国有"友好城市"关系？如果有，这些城市的中国伙伴城市是哪些？
历史	1. 了解中国历史上重要的历史阶段及年代朝代，如：春秋、战国、秦、汉、唐、明、清等； 2. 了解中国历史上的重大历史事件，如：鸦片战争、新中国成立等； 3. 了解中国历史上一些著名历史人物，如：秦始皇、唐太宗、屈原、孔子、司马迁、毛泽东等。	1) 与所在国历史相对照，指出中国的重要历史朝代大致相当于所在国哪个历史时期。 2) 你对所在国与中国的交流史了解多少？试举例说明。
当代中国	1. 了解当代中国金融的基本状况：几家大的银行、股票与基金、外资银行等； 2. 了解中国经济发展的基本特点； 3. 了解中国农村的基本现状：南方与北方、东部与西部差别较大、农民工进城打工等； 4. 了解中国存在的地区间差异及城乡差异概况：东部比西部发展快；城市比农村发展快；城乡差别大；工业带来的环境污染问题。	1) 调查一下儿所在国有没有在中国投资的金融机构，并了解他们为什么在中国投资。 2) 对比说明所在国与中国经济发展的基本特点有什么不同。 3) 说说所在国的农村跟中国的农村有何不同。 4) 所在国存在城乡差异问题吗？

题 材	学 习 任 务	跨文化交际思考问题举例
文学戏剧	1. 知道中国四大名著的名称并了解其故事梗概； 2. 知道一些有名的现当代文学家姓名，并了解一些名著的故事梗概； 3. 京剧的历史与发展。	1) 说出一些与所学中国著名作家同期的所在国文学家的名字及其代表作。 2) 京剧和所在国的戏剧有什么不同？
旅游	知道中国一些著名旅游景点的名称并了解其主要景观内容，如：桂林的山水、西安的兵马俑、北京的故宫和长城等。	你能说出一些跟所在国相似的旅游景点么？它们分别跟所在国的哪些景点相似？具体表现是什么？
风俗	1. 了解一些著名旅游景点的风俗习惯，如云南的少数民族对山歌、舞蹈及文化等； 2. 理解中国人尊老爱幼的优良传统； 3. 了解中国男尊女卑的历史传统以及现在提倡男女平等的现状； 4. 了解中国目前的黄金周及其带来的社会影响：国庆节长假、旅游热和消费热等。	1) 调查一下儿当地的华裔有哪些与所在国不同的风俗习惯。 2) 所在国对待老人跟中国对待老人有些什么不同的观念？你对世界人口老龄化现象的看法？ 3) 所在国是否存在男女不平等的问题？你怎么看待实际生活中的男女不平等问题？ 4) 所在国有类似于黄金周的节假日吗？如果有，在这些节假日里，人们主要有哪些活动？
饮食	1. 了解中国烹饪的方法：煎、炒、烹、炸、烤等； 2. 了解中国人的饮食习惯：南甜北咸；南方米饭、北方面食；合餐习惯等。	1) 说说所在国跟中国的烹饪方法有哪些不同？ 2) 你对中国的合餐习惯有什么看法？请结合所在国的饮食习惯，说说它们的优缺点。

题　材	学　习　任　务	跨文化交际思考问题举例
物产	1. 了解并学习几味常见中药的名字和基本特性，如：薄荷、性寒、性热等； 2. 了解中国几种常见的名茶及其产地：龙井、铁观音等； 3. 了解中国几种常见的名酒，如：茅台、青岛啤酒等。	1) 你对中药和西药有什么不同的看法？ 2) 中国的酒文化和所在国的酒文化有什么不同？

附录四　汉语教学任务活动示范列表

一级在校学习者部分

课程内容		问　候	
活动计划	前期准备	准备一些不同颜色、种类、大小的人物图片和一些写着家庭成员、朋友及问候语句的汉字卡片。	
	主题活动	1. 问候	向不同的人（由同学扮演）问候。
		2. 唱问候歌曲	1) 学习并试唱问候歌曲； 2) 以汉字（或拼音）写出歌词。
	学习成果评估	听——在教师的指导下，试辨出不同的问候语； 说——在教师的指导下，说出简单的问候语； 读——在教师的指导下，试读所学的基本汉字和拼音； 写——在教师的指导下，写出所学的汉字和拼音。	

一级社会学习者部分

课程内容		问　候
活动计划	前期准备	1. 准备一些不同颜色、种类、大小的大家熟悉的公众人物图片，注上人物的名字、称谓（包括汉字和拼音）； 2. 准备一些写着家庭成员、办公室成员、朋友称谓的汉字胸卡； 3. 从几个词中选出正确的放（或抄写）在图片的旁边； 4. 准备一张写着多种问候语句的挂图挂在黑板上。

课程内容		问　　候	
活动计划	主题活动	1. 问好	在一次聚会上，向不同的公众人物（由同学扮演，手中举着人物图片）表示问候。
		2. 拜访	1) 表演到朋友家做客，和朋友的家人（胸前别着胸卡）互相问候。如："王先生，您好！""李小姐，你好！"
			2) 表演到公司拜访，向人问候。如："你好，李小姐。""再见，李先生。"
	成果评估	听——试辨出不同的问候语； 说——试说出简单的问候语； 读——认读所学的表示问候的基本汉字； 写——写出所学的表示问候的基本汉字。	

二级在校学习者部分

课程内容		我的狗	
活动计划	前期准备	准备一些不同颜色、大小的狗的图片和一些颜色及形容语句的汉字卡片。	
	主题活动	1. 认狗	1) 在教师的指导下，说出不同颜色的狗；
			2) 在教师的指导下，说出不同大小的狗；
			3) 在教师的指导下，做出最简单的描述。
		2. 为狗图片着色	为狗图片着色。
活动计划	学习成果评估	听——试听出一些形容语词； 说——试说狗的大与小、不同的颜色； 读——试读出规定的基本汉字； 写——写出所学的基本汉字。	

二级社会学习者部分

课程内容		作息时间表	
活动计划	前期准备	1. 准备一个闹钟； 2. 准备一些时间卡片； 3. 准备一些写着各种活动、地点的卡片； 4. 准备一张简单的作息时间表挂在墙上。	
	主题活动	1. 指认时间	1) 在教师的指导下，学生说出时间； 2) 在教师的指导下，学生说出不同的时间。
		2. 美好的早晨	1) 问答练习； 2) 老师用不同的时间卡片问学生起床、吃早饭、上班等的时间。
		3. 一天的安排	1) 在教师的指导下，学生说出不同的时间； 2) 叙述：按照作息时间表，将一天的安排复述出来。
	成果评估	听——在教师的指导下，听出表示时间、活动的词语； 说——发音准确，掌握四声，并做出简单描述； 读——认读规定的表示活动的汉字； 写——能正确写出规定的表示活动的汉字。	

三级在校学习者部分

课程内容		购　　物
活动计划	前期准备	查阅一些商品的名称和价格，准备一些写着商品名称、人民币价格的卡片、图片或实物。

课程内容	购　　物		
活动计划	主题活动	1. 买东西	1) 指认想要购买的商品。如："我要这个。""我买牛奶。" 2) 询问商品的价格、名称。如："这是什么？""多少钱？" 3) 回答买还是不买。如："要一个。""不要了，谢谢。"
		2. 卖东西	1) 问候。如："你好！" 2) 询问顾客要购买什么商品。如："您买什么？" 3) 介绍商品（名称、价格等）。如："这是毛笔。""五块钱。""一共多少钱？""给你 20 块。"以及关于找零钱等的常用句子。 4) 表示感谢。如："给您，谢谢。" 5) 道别。如："再见！"
	学习成果评估	1. 看一看今天谁买的东西最多？都买了什么？多少钱？ 2. 写一份购物单，并记录所购物品及价钱。	

三级社会学习者部分

课程内容	就　　餐	
活动计划	前期准备	1. 准备一些菜肴、饮料、主食的图片； 2. 准备一张菜单，写着饭菜、饮料的名称、价格； 3. 准备一些写有人民币价格的卡片。
	主题活动	1. 在食堂

请一些同学来表演在食堂就餐。
1) 问候。如："你好！"
2) 指认食物。如："您要什么？""我要这个。"
3) 询问。如："要咖啡吗？"

75

课程内容			就　餐
活动计划	主题活动	2. 在饭馆	请一些同学来表演在饭馆就餐，其他同学记录他们都点了哪些菜。 1) 迎接。如："欢迎。""请坐。""你们几位？" 2) 点餐。如："一份沙拉。""两瓶果汁。" 3) 结账。如："一共 20 块。" 4) 道别。如："再见！"
	成果评估		1. 能说出所点菜的名称和价格； 2. 能说出简单的菜名、钱数等； 3. 能读懂价格和简单的菜谱； 4. 能写出物品的价格。

四级在校学习者部分

课程内容			购　物
活动计划	前期准备		1. 查阅一些商品在不同商店的价格； 2. 准备一些商品的图片或实物； 3. 布置一个小柜台。
	主题活动	1. 买东西	1) 要求拿过商品看一看。如："请拿一下儿那个。""给我看看那件毛衣。" 2) 询问商品的价格、颜色、号码等。如："这个多少钱？""有白色的吗？""有小号的吗？" 3) 简单地评价商品。如："有点儿贵。""大了点儿。" 4) 决定买还是不买。如："要一件。""不要了，谢谢。"
		2. 卖东西	1) 问候与迎接。如："你好！""欢迎光临！" 2) 询问顾客要购买什么商品。
	学习成果评估		将所买商品带回家，请家人评论。

四级社会学习者部分

课程内容	购　　物		
活动计划	前期准备	1. 查阅一些服装在不同商店的价格； 2. 准备一些服装的图片或实物； 3. 布置一个小柜台。	
	主题活动	1. 买衣服	1) 要求拿过商品看一看。如："请拿一下儿那个。""给我看看那件毛衣。" 2) 询问商品的价格、颜色、号码。如："这个多少钱？""有白色的吗？""有小号的吗？" 3) 简单地评价商品。如："有点儿贵。""大了点儿。" 4) 决定买还是不买。如："要一件。""不要了，谢谢。"
		2. 卖衣服	1) 问候与迎接。如："你好！""欢迎光临！""想买点什么？" 2) 询问顾客要购买什么商品。
	成果评估	1. 将新买的衣服穿上，请同学或朋友们评论； 2. 写一个商品报价单。	

五级在校学习者部分

课程内容	报　　名
活动计划	前期准备	1. 查询所要报的旅行团（学习班、俱乐部）的广告； 2. 准备一张旅游地图； 3. 准备一张报名表； 4. 准备身份证、驾驶执照。

国际汉语教学通用课程大纲

课程内容	报 名		
活动计划	主题活动	1. 与人商量	1) 说明意图。如："我想假期报个团去中国旅游。" 2) 表示态度（赞成、犹豫或反对）并说明理由。如："太好了，我也正想去中国看看呢。听说随团旅游很便宜。" 3) 商议或争执。如："这个季节南京太热了，不如去东北。""选哪家旅行社比较好？"
		2. 办理报名手续	1) 填交报名表。如："请您用钢笔填写。""请填上详细的通讯地址。" 2) 办手续（照相、签字、盖章、交费）。如："请您在这里签一下儿名。""等签证下来我们会通知您。" 3) 签合同。如："请您再仔细看一遍合同，有没有异议？""旅游保险包括进去了吗？"
	学习成果评估	1. 做一个详细的旅行计划； 2. 能听懂入关时的简单问话； 3. 能回答简单的问话； 4. 能读懂一些旅行注意事项； 5. 能填写简单的表格。	

五级社会学习者部分

课程内容	加入俱乐部	
活动计划	前期准备	1. 准备几张俱乐部的广告； 2. 准备几张俱乐部活动的图片； 3. 准备一张报名表。

78

课程内容	加入俱乐部		
活动计划	主题活动	1. 商量	1) 说明意图。如："我想加入篮球俱乐部。"
			2) 表示态度（赞成、犹豫或反对）。如："太好了，我也正想报名呢。"
			3) 商议或争执。如："你不如加入我们合唱团。"
		2. 办手续	1) 咨询。如："请问，每周活动几次？"
			2) 宣传。如："我们在上次联赛中获得了第二名。"
			3) 填交报名表。如："请填上您的联系方式。"
			4) 办手续（交费、签字）。如："请您在这里签一下儿名。"
		3. 入队	1) 欢迎新会员仪式，介绍每个会员的特点。
			2) 相互认识。
		4. 比赛	1) 看一次比赛的录像。
			2) 组织一次队内的比赛。
	成果评估	1. 写一份俱乐部的情况介绍；	
		2. 能听懂人们在特定场合的相互介绍与称呼；	
		3. 能说明自己加入俱乐部的原因；	
		4. 写一篇体育比赛的报道。	

附录五 常用汉语语法项目分级表

一级语法项目表

目标 描述	了解和掌握： 1. 基本语序 2. 常用句型 3. 一般疑问句 4. 数词和常用量词 5. 人称代词 6. 指示代词 7. 常用程度副词 8. 描述人和物的基本表达方式 9. 用"不"的否定句	

	语法项目	**结构形式**	**例　句**
内容	1. 动词谓语句	主语＋动词＋宾语	我姓王。
	1.1 "是"字句	主语＋是＋宾语	玛丽是美国人。
	1.2 "有"字句	主语＋有＋宾语	我有一个弟弟。
		主语＋没有＋宾语	我没有电子词典。
	2. 用"吗"、"吧"、"呢" 的一般疑问句	小句＋吗?	玛丽是大学生吗?
		小句＋吧?	约翰是美国人吧?
		小句,名词/代词＋呢?	我是中国人，你呢?

语法项目	结构形式	例　句
3. 形容词谓语句	主语＋副词＋形容词	我很高兴。 玛丽非常漂亮。
4. 名词谓语句	主语＋年龄／籍贯等	玛丽 20 岁。 王明上海人。
5. 用"不"的否定句	主语＋不＋动词短语	我不喜欢唱歌。
6. 祈使句：表示礼貌请求	请＋动词！	请进！ 请坐！
7. 感叹句	真＋形容词！	真好！
	太＋形容词＋了！	太棒了！
8. 人称代词	你、我、他、她、您	您贵姓？
8.1 复数人称代词	你们、我们、他们	我们学习汉语。
8.2 指示代词	这、那	这位是布朗先生。 那个人是美国人。
9. 程度副词作状语	很、非常、真、太	布朗非常忙。
10. 数词	1~100	我爸爸 66 岁。
11. 常用量词	个、名	我家有两个男孩。 我们班有 25 名学生。
12. 连词	A 和 B	我和弟弟 爸爸、妈妈和我

内容

二级语法项目表

目标描述	了解和掌握： 1. 时间、地点、方位的基本表达方式 2. 人民币、钱数 3. 状语、定语的基本结构和功能 4. 特殊疑问句 5. 表示存在的方式 6. 表示意愿的方式		
	语法项目	**结构形式**	**例　句**
内容	1. 时间名词		
	1.1 年、月、日的表达	__年__月__日	2007 年 12 月 5 日
	1.2 星期的表达	星期__	星期一～星期天
	1.3 时点的表达	__点__分	8 点、8 点 10 分
		差__分__点	差 5 分 8 点 差 1 刻 10 点
	2. 人民币钱数的表达	__元 / 块__角 / 毛__分	105 块 6 角 8 分
	3. 名词谓语句	主语＋时间	今天 12 月 6 号。 明天星期四。 现在 9 点 20。
		主语＋钱数	这本书 32 块 5 毛。 3 斤苹果 10 块钱。

语法项目	结构形式	例　句
4. 时间状语	主语＋时间状语＋动词短语	我每天早上6点半起床。
5. 地点状语	主语＋在＋地点／处所＋动词短语	我在一家电脑公司工作。
6. 所属关系的表达	名词／代词＋（的）＋名词	这是我的书。 她是我弟弟。
7．方位词		
7.1 简单方位词	上、下、左、右、前、后、东、西、南、北、中	
7.2 合成方位词	简单方位词＋面／边	上面、上边、东面、东边、西面、西边
7.3 方位词组	处所名词＋简单方位词＋（面／边）	桌子上、窗外、银行前边、学校西边
8. 用疑问代词的特殊疑问句	什么、谁、哪、哪儿、几、多少、多大、什么时候	你叫什么名字？ 他是谁？ 你是哪国人？ 你在哪儿上学？ 现在几点了？ 你的孩子多大了？ 这本书多少钱？ 你什么时候开学？
9. 存在的表达		

内容

语法项目	结构形式	例 句
9.1 "在"字句	方位词（词组）+ 在 + 方位词组	北京大学在清华大学西边。
9.2 "有"字句	方位词组 + 有 + 名词（词组）	桌子上有两本书。
9.3 "是"字句	方位词组 + 是 + 名词（词组）	图书馆西边是运动场。
10. 距离的表达	A 点 + 离 +B 点 + 远 / 近 / 距离数	北京大学离清华大学很近。
11. 意愿的表达："要"、"想"	主语 + 要 + 名词	我要一瓶可乐。
	主语 + 要 / 想 + 动词短语	我想去中国。玛丽要去图书馆。
12. "的"字结构	名词 / 代词 + 的	这是玛丽的。
	形容词 + 的	红的好看。
13. 动词重叠和动词 + 一下儿	动词重叠	我试试这件衣服。
	动词 + 一下儿	你看一下儿这本书。
14. 常用量词	件、条、块、张、斤	一件衬衣、两条裤子、三块面包、四张桌子、五斤苹果
15. 范围副词作状语		

内容

84

	语法项目	结构形式	例　句
内容	15.1 都	都 + 动词短语	我们都学习汉语。
	15.2 也	也 + 动词短语	他也是美国人。

三级语法项目表

目标描述	了解和掌握： 1. 常用介词 2. 基本比较句 3. 描述事件或行为正在进行的表达方式 4. 助词"了"的基本用法 5. 用"没（有）"的否定句 6. 常用能愿动词

	语法项目	结构形式	例　句
内容	1. 介词：引进空间方位作状语		
	1.1 从	从 + 起点 + 动词短语	我刚从英国回来。
	1.2 向	向 + 方向 + 动词短语	（你）一直向北走。
	1.3 往	往 + 方向 + 动词短语	往右拐。
	1.4 从……到……	从 + 起点 + 到 + 终点	从这儿到你们大学怎么走？
	2. 事件正在进行的表达	主语 + 正 + 动词短语 + 呢	布朗正看书呢。

语法项目	结构形式	例　句
	主语 + 在 + 动词短语 +（呢）	玛丽在睡觉（呢）。
	主语 + 正在 + 动词短语 +（呢）	王先生正在打电话(呢)。
3. 助词"着"的用法	主语 + 动词 + 着 + 名词	布朗戴着一副眼镜。
4. 存现句	方位词组 + 动词 + 着 + 名词（词组）	墙上挂着一张世界地图。
5. 助词"了"的用法	数量词 / 名词 + 了	我儿子 8 岁了。 秋天了。
	主语 + 形容词 / 动词 + 了	花红了。 玛丽病了。
	小句 + 了	我昨天去王府井了。
	主语 + 动词 + 了 + 数量 / 动量 +（名）	我买了两件衬衫。 这本书我看了两遍。
6. 用"没（有）"的否定句	主语 + 没（有）+ 动词短语	我没有看电视。
7. 类同的表达	…… 跟 / 和 ……（不）一样	我跟你不一样。
	…… 跟 / 和 ……（不）一样 + 形容词	他和我一样高。

内容

86

语法项目	结构形式	例 句
8. 比较句		
8.1 "比"字句	A + 比 + B + 形容词	今天比昨天冷。
8.2 "比"字句的否定	A + 没有 + B + 形容词	你没有玛丽高。
9. 副词"最"	最 + 形容词 / 动词短语	这是中国最大的城市。
10. 双宾语句	主语 + 直接宾语 + 间接宾语	玛丽给我一本书。 找你两块钱。
11. 连动句	主语 + 动词短语 1 + 动词短语 2	我坐地铁去上班。 我用筷子吃饭。
12. 选择疑问句	……还是……？	你喝茶还是喝咖啡？ 你去还是我去？
13. 正反疑问句	主语 + Adj. 不 Adj.？	那件衣服贵不贵？
	主语 + V 不 V +（宾语）？	你来不来？
	主语 + V 没 V +（宾语）？	你看没看电影？
14. 用"怎么"询问方式	主语 + 怎么 + 动词短语？	这个字怎么念？ 去银行怎么走？
15. 用"怎么样？"、"好吗？"、"可以吗？"、"行吗？"的疑问句	名词词组 + 怎么样？	这本汉语书怎么样？

内容

87

语法项目	结构形式	例　句
	小句，怎么样？	我们坐公共汽车去，怎么样？
	小句，好吗？	我们吃中餐，好吗？
	小句，可以吗？	我这样说，可以吗？
	小句，行吗？	这样写，行吗？
16. 能愿动词		
16.1 能	能＋动词短语	玛丽能来。
16.2 会	会＋动词短语	我会打网球。
16.3 可以	可以＋动词短语	这儿可以拍照。
16.4 应该	应该＋动词短语	你应该早点儿来。
16.5 愿意	愿意＋动词短语	我愿意学习汉语。
17. 介词：引进对象作状语		
17.1 跟	跟＋某人（一起）＋动词短语	我跟他一起去。
17.2 给	给＋某人＋动词短语	我给爸爸打电话。

内容

四级语法项目表

目标描述	了解和掌握： 1. 常用时间副词 2. 助词"过"的用法 3. 时量补语 4. 动量补语 5. "是……的"句的用法 6. 兼语句 7. 常用复句		
内容	**语法项目**	**结构形式**	**例　句**
	1. 时间副词作状语： 1.1 还	还 + 动词短语	玛丽还在看电视。 他们还没下班呢。
	1.2 已经	已经 + 动词短语	他们已经下班了。
	1.3 再和又	主语 + 再 + 动词短语	你再听一遍。
		主语 + 又 + 动词短语	他又说了一遍。
	1.4 就和才	主语 +（时间）+ 就 + 动词短语	我就来。 我今天6点就起床了。
		主语 +（时间）+ 才 + 动词短语	他才来。 他今天8点半才来上班。
	2. 助词"了"的用法	该 + 名词短语 / 动词短语 + 了	该你了。 该上课了。

	语法项目	结构形式	例 句
内容		（就／快）要＋动词短语＋了	快要下雨了。 飞机就要起飞了。
		能愿动词＋动词短语＋了	我能走了。 我会说汉语了。 你可以下班了。
		不＋动词短语＋了	我不去了。 他不喝酒了。
		主语＋动词＋了＋名词＋就／再＋动词短语	我吃了饭再去。 我下了课就来你这儿了。
	3. 助词"过"的用法	主语＋（没）＋动词＋过＋名词（短语）	我去过中国。 我没看过这部电影。
	4. 时量补语	动词＋时量	我吃过两次烤鸭。
		动词短语＋时量＋了	我来北京三年了。 他大学毕业 10 年了。
		动词＋了＋时量＋（名词）	我打了两个小时网球。
		动词＋了＋时量＋（名词）＋了	我打了两个小时网球了。
	5. 动量补语		
	5.1 次	动词＋数＋次	我去过三次上海。

	语法项目	结构形式	例　句
内容	5.2 遍	动词 + 数 + 遍	这本书我看过三遍。
	5.3 趟	动词 + 数 + 趟	我去了一趟香港。
	6. 比较句	A + 比 + B + 更 / 还 + 形容词	今天比昨天还冷。
		A + 比 + B + 形容词 + 数量	我比我弟弟大三岁。
		A + 比 + B + 形容词 + 一点儿 / 多了	他的汉语比我好多了。
	7. 兼语句	主语 + 请 / 让 / 叫 / + 某人 + 动词短语	我请王老师看电影。 妈妈不让我抽烟。
	8.特殊句式：是……的		
	8.1 强调时间	主语 + 是 + 时间 + 动词短语 + 的	我是 1968 年出生的。
	8.2 强调空间方位	主语 + 是 + 空间方位 + 动词短语 + 的	我是在北京出生的。 他是从美国来的。
	8.3 强调方式	主语 + 是 + 方式 + 动词短语 + 的	他是坐飞机来的。
	9. 用"怎么了"的疑问句	名词 + 怎么了？	你怎么了？

	语法项目	结构形式	例　句
内容	10. 复句	先……，再……	你先写作业，一会儿再看电视。
		因为……，所以……	因为很忙，所以我没去。
		如果（要是）……，就……	要是下雨，我们就不去了。
		不但……，而且……	他不但学习汉语，而且还学习西班牙语。
		虽然……，但是……	虽然很累，但是我一定要完成作业。

五级语法项目表

目标描述	了解和掌握： 1. 结果补语、趋向补语、可能补语、程度补语 2. "把"字句 3. 汉语被动意义的表达 4. 各种复句		
	语法项目	**结构形式**	**例　句**
内容	1. 结果补语		
	1.1 一般形容词作结果补语	动词＋形容词	衣服洗干净了。
	1.2 "完"作结果补语	动词＋完	作业写完了。

	语法项目	结构形式	例　句
内容	1.3 "到"作结果补语	动词 + 到	飞机票买到了。
	1.4 "好"作结果补语	动词 + 好	晚饭做好了。
	1.5 结果补语的否定	没 + 动词 + 结果补语	晚饭还没做好。
	2. 结果补语的可能式		
	2.1 肯定的可能式	动词 + 得 + 补语 或 能 + 动词 + 补语	这么多作业，你写得完吗？ 我能买到去上海的飞机票。
	2.2 否定的可能式	动词 + 不 + 补语	这么多作业，我写不完。
	3. 常用的可能补语	看得见 / 看不见	飞机看不见了。
		睡得着 / 睡不着	我睡不着。
		动词 + 得 / 不 + 了	明天的课我上不了。
	4. 趋向补语		
	4.1 简单趋向补语	动词 + 来 / 去	上来、上去、下来、下去、进来、进去、出来、出去、过来、过去、回来、回去、起来
	4.2 复合趋向补语	动词 + 上 / 下 + 来 / 去	拿上来、搬下去
		动词 + 进 / 出 + 来 / 去	跑进来、走出去

语法项目	结构形式	例 句
	动词 + 回 + 来 / 去	走回来、寄回去
	动词 + 过 + 来 / 去	跳过来、跳过去
	动词 + 起 + 来	站起来
4.3 趋向补语的引申用法	动词 + 上	关上窗户
	动词 + 下	脱下大衣
	动词 + 起来	笑起来、做起来
	动词 + 下去	说下去
4.4 趋向补语的可能式	动词 + 得 / 不 + 趋向补语	进得来、进不来 拿得起来、拿不起来
5. 程度补语		
5.1 程度补语	动词 + 得 + 程度副词 + 形容词	玛丽跑得很快。 我今天吃得不太多。
5.2 动词受事在程度补语的位置	施事 + 动词 + 受事 + 动词 + 得 + 形容词	玛丽说汉语说得很好。
	施事 + 受事 + 动词 + 得 + 形容词	玛丽篮球打得不太好。
	受事 + 施事 + 动词 + 得 + 形容词	这首歌玛丽唱得很好听。

内容

语法项目	结构形式	例　句
6."把"字句	主语＋把＋名词＋动词＋补充成分	
	主语＋把＋名词＋动词＋形容词	我把房间打扫干净了。
	主语＋把＋名词＋动词＋趋向	你把铅笔递过来。
	主语＋把＋名词＋动词＋在＋地方	我把车停在学校门口了。
	主语＋把＋名词＋动词＋到＋地方	请你把我的包拿到205房间。
	主语＋把＋名词＋动词＋给＋某人	他把这封信交给了玛丽。
7. 被动意义的表达		
7.1 意义上的被动句	受事＋动词＋补充成分	作业写完了。 这顿饭吃得很香。
7.2 "被"字句	受事＋被（＋施事）＋动词＋补充成分	我的腿被守门员撞伤了。
	受事＋是＋施事＋动词＋的	这本书是马老师编的。

内容

95

	语法项目	结构形式	例　句
内容	8.各种复句	既然……就……	既然这么贵，我就不买了。
		即使……也……	即使再贵点儿，我也要买。
		无论……都……	无论多远，我都要去。
		不是……就是……	周末他不是睡懒觉就是出去玩。
		宁可……也……	我宁可饿死，也不吃这种菜。

附录六 汉语拼音声母、韵母与声调

一、声母

声　母	国际音标	声　母	国际音标
b	[p]	j	[tɕ]
p	[p']	q	[tɕ']
m	[m]	x	[ɕ]
f	[f]	zh	[tʂ]
d	[t]	ch	[tʂ']
t	[t']	sh	[ʂ]
n	[n]	r	[ʐ]
l	[l]	z	[ts]
g	[k]	c	[ts']
k	[k']	s	[s]
h	[x]		

二、韵母

韵　母	国际音标	韵　母	国际音标
a	[A]	iang	[iɑŋ]
o	[o]	ing	[iŋ]
e	[ɤ]	iong	[yŋ]
ai	[ai]	u②	[u]
ei	[ei]	ua	[uA]
ao	[ɑu]	uo	[uo]
ou	[ou]	uai	[uai]
an	[an]	ui, uei	[uei]
en	[ən]	uan	[uan]
ang	[ɑŋ]	un, uen	[uən]

韵　母	国际音标	韵　母	国际音标
eng	[əŋ]	uang	[uɑŋ]
ong	[uŋ]	ueng	[uəŋ]
i①	[i]	ü③	[y]
ia	[iA]	üe	[yɛ]
ie	[iɛ]	üan	[yan]
iao	[iau]	ün	[yn]
iu, iou	[iou]	-i④	[ɿ], [ʅ]
ian	[iæn]	ê	[ɛ]
in	[in]	er	[ɚ]

① i 行韵母前面没有声母时，分别写成 yi，ya，ye，yao，you，yan，yin，yang，ying，yong。

② u 行韵母前面没有声母时，分别写成 wu，wa，wo，wai，wei，wan，wen，wang，weng。

③ ü 行韵母前面没有声母时，分别写成 yu，yue，yuan，yun。ü 上的两点省略。

④ zh，ch，sh，r，z，c，s 的韵母用 -i。其中 z，c，s 之后用 [ɿ]，zh，ch，sh，r 之后用 [ʅ]。

三、声调符号

阴　平	阳　平	上　声	去　声	轻　声
－	∕	∨	＼	
妈	麻	马	骂	吗
mā	má	mǎ	mà	ma

附录七　常用汉语800字表

A							
阿	ā	啊	à	啊	a	爱	ài
安	ān						

B							
八	bā	巴	bā	吧	bā	把	bǎ
把	bà	爸	bà	吧	ba	白	bái
百	bǎi	班	bān	板	bǎn	办	bàn
半	bàn	帮	bāng	包	bāo	饱	bǎo
宝	bǎo	保	bǎo	报	bào	抱	bào
杯	bēi	北	běi	备	bèi	被	bèi
本	běn	鼻	bí	比	bǐ	笔	bǐ
币	bì	必	bì	边	biān	变	biàn
便	biàn	表	biǎo	别	bié	病	bìng
不	bù	布	bù	步	bù	部	bù

C							
擦	cā	才	cái	财	cái	菜	cài
参	cān	餐	cān	草	cǎo	层	céng
差	chā	茶	chá	查	chá	察	chá
差	chà	产	chǎn	长	cháng	场	cháng
常	cháng	厂	chǎng	场	chǎng	唱	chàng
朝	cháo	吵	chǎo	车	chē	晨	chén
成	chéng	城	chéng	吃	chī	持	chí
重	chóng	丑	chǒu	出	chū	初	chū
除	chú	处	chǔ	处	chù	穿	chuān
传	chuán	船	chuán	窗	chuāng	床	chuáng
吹	chuī	春	chūn	词	cí	次	cì
从	cóng	村	cūn	存	cún	错	cuò

D							
答	dá	打	dǎ	大	dà	代	dài
带	dài	待	dài	单	dān	但	dàn
蛋	dàn	当	dāng	当	dàng	刀	dāo

导	dǎo	倒	dǎo	到	dào	倒	dào
道	dào	得	dé	地	de	的	de
得	de	灯	dēng	等	děng	低	dī
的	dí	地	dì	弟	dì	的	dì
第	dì	典	diǎn	点	diǎn	电	diàn
店	diàn	调	diào	订	dìng	定	dìng
东	dōng	冬	dōng	懂	dǒng	动	dòng
都	dōu	都	dū	毒	dú	读	dú
度	dù	短	duǎn	对	duì	顿	dùn
多	duō						

E

阿	ē	饿	è	儿	ér	耳	ěr
二	èr						

F

发	fā	法	fǎ	发	fà	烦	fán
反	fǎn	饭	fàn	方	fāng	房	fáng
访	fǎng	放	fàng	飞	fēi	非	fēi
肥	féi	费	fèi	分	fēn	分	fèn
丰	fēng	风	fēng	夫	fū	服	fú
福	fú	府	fǔ	父	fù	负	fù
复	fù	富	fù				

G

该	gāi	改	gǎi	干	gān	赶	gǎn
敢	gǎn	感	gǎn	干	gàn	刚	gāng
高	gāo	搞	gǎo	告	gào	哥	gē
歌	gē	格	gé	个	gè	各	gè
给	gěi	根	gēn	跟	gēn	更	gēng
更	gèng	工	gōng	公	gōng	宫	gōng
共	gòng	狗	gǒu	够	gòu	姑	gū
古	gǔ	股	gǔ	故	gù	顾	gù
刮	guā	挂	guà	关	guān	观	guān
馆	guǎn	管	guǎn	观	guàn	广	guǎng
贵	guì	国	guó	果	guǒ	过	guò

H

还	hái	孩	hái	海	hǎi	喊	hǎn

汉	hàn	行	háng	航	háng	好	hǎo
号	hào	好	hào	喝	hē	合	hé
何	hé	和	hé	河	hé	黑	hēi
很	hěn	红	hóng	后	hòu	候	hòu
胡	hú	湖	hú	互	hù	户	hù
护	hù	花	huā	华	huá	化	huà
划	huà	画	huà	话	huà	坏	huài
欢	huān	还	huán	环	huán	换	huàn
皇	huáng	黄	huáng	回	huí	会	huì
婚	hūn	活	huó	火	huǒ		

J

机	jī	鸡	jī	基	jī	及	jí
吉	jí	级	jí	极	jí	急	jí
集	jí	几	jǐ	己	jǐ	挤	jǐ
给	jǐ	计	jì	记	jì	技	jì
系	jì	际	jì	济	jì	寄	jì
加	jiā	家	jiā	假	jiǎ	驾	jià
架	jià	假	jià	间	jiān	检	jiǎn
简	jiǎn	见	jiàn	件	jiàn	间	jiàn
建	jiàn	健	jiàn	江	jiāng	将	jiāng
讲	jiǎng	将	jiàng	交	jiāo	教	jiāo
角	jiǎo	饺	jiǎo	脚	jiǎo	叫	jiào
觉	jiào	校	jiào	较	jiào	教	jiào
接	jiē	街	jiē	节	jié	结	jié
姐	jiě	解	jiě	介	jiè	界	jiè
借	jiè	斤	jīn	今	jīn	金	jīn
紧	jǐn	进	jìn	近	jìn	京	jīng
经	jīng	精	jīng	警	jǐng	净	jìng
静	jìng	九	jiǔ	久	jiǔ	酒	jiǔ
旧	jiù	就	jiù	居	jū	局	jú
举	jǔ	巨	jù	具	jù	剧	jù
决	jué	觉	jué				

K

卡	kǎ	开	kāi	看	kān	看	kàn
康	kāng	考	kǎo	科	kē	可	kě

渴	kě	克	kè	刻	kè	客	kè
课	kè	空	kōng	孔	kǒng	空	kòng
口	kǒu	哭	kū	苦	kǔ	裤	kù
块	kuài	快	kuài	筷	kuài	困	kùn
L							
拉	lā	落	là	来	lái	劳	láo
老	lǎo	乐	lè	了	le	累	lěi
累	lèi	冷	lěng	离	lí	礼	lǐ
里	lǐ	理	lǐ	力	lì	历	lì
立	lì	利	lì	例	lì	连	lián
联	lián	脸	liǎn	练	liàn	凉	liáng
粮	liáng	两	liǎng	亮	liàng	凉	liàng
了	liǎo	料	liào	林	lín	零	líng
领	lǐng	另	lìng	留	liú	六	liù
陆	liù	龙	lóng	楼	lóu	陆	lù
录	lù	路	lù	旅	lǚ	律	lǜ
绿	lǜ	乱	luàn	论	lùn	落	luò
M							
妈	mā	麻	má	马	mǎ	吗	ma
买	mǎi	卖	mài	满	mǎn	慢	màn
忙	máng	猫	māo	毛	máo	冒	mào
贸	mào	帽	mào	么	me	没	méi
每	měi	美	měi	妹	mèi	门	mén
们	men	米	mǐ	面	miàn	民	mín
名	míng	明	míng	没	mò	母	mǔ
木	mù	目	mù				
N							
拿	ná	哪	nǎ	那	nà	奶	nǎi
男	nán	南	nán	难	nán	脑	nǎo
呢	ne	内	nèi	能	néng	你	nǐ
年	nián	娘	niáng	鸟	niǎo	您	nín
牛	niú	农	nóng	女	nǚ	暖	nuǎn
O							
欧	ōu						

102

	P						
爬	pá	怕	pà	排	pái	盘	pán
旁	páng	胖	pàng	跑	pǎo	朋	péng
碰	pèng	皮	pí	啤	pí	便	pián
片	piàn	漂	piāo	票	piào	漂	piào
品	pǐn	平	píng	苹	píng	瓶	píng
破	pò						
	Q						
七	qī	期	qī	齐	qí	奇	qí
骑	qí	起	qǐ	气	qì	汽	qì
卡	qiǎ	千	qiān	前	qián	钱	qián
浅	qiǎn	桥	qiáo	切	qiē	切	qiè
亲	qīn	青	qīng	轻	qīng	清	qīng
情	qíng	请	qǐng	秋	qiū	求	qiú
球	qiú	区	qū	取	qǔ	去	qù
全	quán	确	què				
	R						
然	rán	让	ràng	热	rè	人	rén
认	rèn	任	rèn	日	rì	容	róng
肉	ròu	如	rú	入	rù		
	S						
赛	sài	三	sān	散	sǎn	散	sàn
色	sè	沙	shā	厦	shà	山	shān
扇	shàn	伤	shāng	商	shāng	上	shǎng
上	shàng	烧	shāo	少	shǎo	少	shào
绍	shào	舍	shě	社	shè	舍	shè
谁	shéi	申	shēn	身	shēn	参	shēn
深	shēn	什	shén	神	shén	升	shēng
生	shēng	声	shēng	省	shěng	剩	shèng
师	shī	十	shí	石	shí	时	shí
识	shí	实	shí	食	shí	史	shǐ
使	shǐ	始	shǐ	士	shì	示	shì
世	shì	市	shì	事	shì	试	shì
视	shì	适	shì	是	shì	室	shì
收	shōu	熟	shóu	手	shǒu	首	shǒu

受	shòu	售	shòu	书	shū	舒	shū
输	shū	熟	shú	数	shǔ	术	shù
树	shù	数	shù	双	shuāng	谁	shuí
水	shuǐ	睡	shuì	说	shuō	思	sī
死	sǐ	四	sì	寺	sì	送	sòng
诉	sù	宿	sù	酸	suān	算	suàn
随	suí	岁	suì	所	suǒ		

			T				
他	tā	它	tā	她	tā	台	tái
太	tài	谈	tán	汤	tāng	堂	táng
糖	táng	躺	tǎng	疼	téng	梯	tī
提	tí	题	tí	体	tǐ	天	tiān
甜	tián	填	tián	条	tiáo	调	tiáo
跳	tiào	听	tīng	停	tíng	通	tōng
同	tóng	统	tǒng	头	tóu	图	tú
土	tǔ	团	tuán	推	tuī	腿	tuǐ
退	tuì	脱	tuō				

			W				
袜	wà	外	wài	完	wán	玩	wán
晚	wǎn	碗	wǎn	万	wàn	王	wáng
网	wǎng	往	wǎng	忘	wàng	望	wàng
危	wēi	为	wéi	卫	wèi	为	wèi
位	wèi	喂	wèi	温	wēn	文	wén
闻	wén	问	wèn	我	wǒ	握	wò
无	wú	五	wǔ	午	wǔ	舞	wǔ
务	wù	物	wù	误	wù		

			X				
西	xī	希	xī	息	xī	习	xí
洗	xǐ	喜	xǐ	系	xì	细	xì
下	xià	夏	xià	先	xiān	险	xiǎn
现	xiàn	相	xiāng	香	xiāng	响	xiǎng
想	xiǎng	向	xiàng	像	xiàng	消	xiāo
销	xiāo	小	xiǎo	校	xiào	笑	xiào
些	xiē	鞋	xié	写	xiě	谢	xiè
心	xīn	新	xīn	信	xìn	兴	xīng

星	xīng	行	xíng	省	xǐng	兴	xìng
幸	xìng	性	xìng	姓	xìng	休	xiū
须	xū	需	xū	许	xǔ	学	xué
雪	xuě	血	xuè				

呀	yā	鸭	yā	牙	yá	亚	yà
呀	ya	言	yán	颜	yán	眼	yǎn
演	yǎn	羊	yáng	阳	yáng	样	yàng
要	yāo	要	yào	药	yào	爷	yé
也	yě	业	yè	页	yè	夜	yè
一	yī	衣	yī	医	yī	宜	yí
已	yǐ	以	yǐ	椅	yǐ	亿	yì
义	yì	艺	yì	议	yì	易	yì
意	yì	因	yīn	阴	yīn	音	yīn
银	yín	应	yīng	英	yīng	迎	yíng
影	yǐng	应	yìng	永	yǒng	用	yòng
优	yōu	邮	yóu	油	yóu	游	yóu
友	yǒu	有	yǒu	又	yòu	右	yòu
鱼	yú	雨	yǔ	语	yǔ	育	yù
元	yuán	园	yuán	员	yuán	原	yuán
远	yuǎn	院	yuàn	愿	yuàn	月	yuè
乐	yuè	越	yuè	云	yún		

灾	zāi	再	zài	在	zài	咱	zán
脏	zāng	脏	zàng	早	zǎo	责	zé
怎	zěn	增	zēng	展	zhǎn	站	zhàn
张	zhāng	章	zhāng	长	zhǎng	掌	zhǎng
账	zhàng	着	zhāo	朝	zhāo	着	zháo
找	zhǎo	照	zhào	者	zhě	这	zhè
着	zhe	真	zhēn	正	zhēng	正	zhèng
证	zhèng	政	zhèng	之	zhī	支	zhī
只	zhī	汁	zhī	知	zhī	直	zhí
只	zhǐ	纸	zhǐ	指	zhǐ	至	zhì
志	zhì	制	zhì	治	zhì	中	zhōng
钟	zhōng	中	zhòng	众	zhòng	重	zhòng

州	zhōu	周	zhōu	洲	zhōu	猪	zhū
主	zhǔ	助	zhù	住	zhù	注	zhù
祝	zhù	传	zhuàn	装	zhuāng	准	zhǔn
桌	zhuō	着	zhuó	子	zǐ	自	zì
字	zì	总	zǒng	走	zǒu	租	zū
足	zú	族	zú	组	zǔ	祖	zǔ
嘴	zuǐ	最	zuì	罪	zuì	昨	zuó
左	zuǒ	作	zuò	坐	zuò	座	zuò
做	zuò						

（引自：《汉语 800 字》编写组. 汉语 800 字. 北京：外语教学与研究出版社，2007）

附录八 常用汉语1500高频词语表

频度	词语	拼音	频度	词语	拼音	频度	词语	拼音
1	的	de			de	55	走	zǒu
2	了	le	29	很	hěn	56	吧	ba
3	我	wǒ	30	我们	wǒmen	57	从	cóng
4	是	shì	31	又	yòu	58	中	zhōng
5	一	yī	32	看	kān			zhòng
6	在	zài			kàn	59	您	nín
7	不	bù	33	要	yào	60	几	jǐ
8	他	tā	34	里	lǐ	61	出	chū
9	你	nǐ			li	62	它	tā
10	有	yǒu	35	还	hái	63	下	xià
11	说	shuō			huán	64	小	xiǎo
12	就	jiù	36	没有	méiyǒu	65	而	ér
13	也	yě	37	把	bǎ	66	知道	zhīdào
14	这	zhè	38	什么	shénme	67	可以	kěyǐ
15	人	rén	39	对	duì	68	用	yòng
16	着	zhe	40	那	nà	69	没	méi
17	都	dōu	41	多	duō	70	时候	shíhou
18	去	qù	42	大	dà	71	最	zuì
19	和	hé	43	想	xiǎng	72	叫	jiào
20	上	shàng	44	给	gěi	73	做	zuò
21	到	dào	45	自己	zìjǐ	74	天	tiān
22	来	lái	46	过	guò	75	只	zhī
23	个	gè	47	他们	tāmen			zhǐ
24	她	tā	48	吗	ma	76	老师	lǎoshī
25	地	de	49	会	huì	77	听	tīng
		dì	50	能	néng	78	为	wéi
26	一个	yīgè	51	两	liǎng			wèi
27	好	hǎo	52	呢	ne	79	再	zài
		hào	53	吃	chī	80	但	dàn
28	得	dé	54	年	nián	81	起来	qǐlái

频度	词语	拼音	频度	词语	拼音	频度	词语	拼音
82	时	shí	112	怎么	zěnme	142	进	jìn
83	才	cái	113	位	wèi	143	当	dāng
84	这个	zhège	114	钱	qián			dàng
85	太	tài	115	跟	gēn	144	话	huà
86	像	xiàng	116	更	gèng	145	朋友	péngyou
87	让	ràng	117	与	yǔ	146	这些	zhèxiē
88	买	mǎi	118	请	qǐng	147	比	bǐ
89	现在	xiànzài	119	生活	shēnghuó	148	笑	xiào
90	却	què	120	四	sì	149	大家	dàjiā
91	这样	zhèyàng	121	父亲	fùqīn	150	成	chéng
92	们	men	122	人们	rénmen	151	开	kāi
93	点	diǎn	123	向	xiàng	152	出来	chūlái
94	真	zhēn	124	打	dǎ	153	一样	yīyàng
95	已经	yǐjing	125	后	hòu	154	并	bìng
96	事	shì	126	还是	háishì	155	妈妈	māma
97	你们	nǐmen	127	先生	xiānsheng	156	月	yuè
98	便	biàn	128	住	zhù	157	母亲	mǔqīn
99	次	cì	129	起	qǐ	158	前	qián
100	问	wèn	130	可是	kěshì	159	但是	dànshì
101	等	děng	131	今天	jīntiān	160	如果	rúguǒ
102	坐	zuò	132	工作	gōngzuò	161	带	dài
103	被	bèi	133	谁	shéi	162	地方	dìfang
104	三	sān	134	见	jiàn	163	还有	háiyǒu
105	可	kě	135	觉得	juéde	164	回	huí
106	种	zhǒng	136	之	zhī	165	书	shū
		zhòng	137	时间	shíjiān	166	快	kuài
107	家	jiā	138	东西	dōngxī	167	一定	yīdìng
108	啊	a			dōngxi	168	喝	hē
109	孩子	háizi	139	写	xiě	169	件	jiàn
110	喜欢	xǐhuan	140	以后	yǐhòu	170	爸爸	bàba
111	因为	yīnwèi	141	拿	ná	171	儿	ér

频度	词语	拼音	频度	词语	拼音	频度	词语	拼音
172	岁	suì	202	站	zhàn	233	有些	yǒuxiē
173	一起	yìqǐ	203	车	chē	234	看看	kànkan
174	找	zhǎo	204	将	jiāng	235	为了	wèile
175	世界	shìjiè	205	先	xiān	236	学生	xuésheng
176	新	xīn	206	于是	yúshì	237	门	mén
177	学习	xuéxí	207	完	wán	238	或	huò
178	长	cháng	208	问题	wèntí	239	一下	yíxià
		zhǎng	209	第一	dìyī	240	以	yǐ
179	所以	suǒyǐ	210	水	shuǐ	241	过去	guòqù
180	学	xué	211	送	sòng	242	死	sǐ
181	手	shǒu	212	忙	máng	243	跑	pǎo
182	非常	fēicháng	213	画	huà	244	这儿	zhèr
183	看见	kànjiàn	214	就是	jiùshì	245	字	zì
184	那么	nàme	215	块	kuài	246	别	bié
185	使	shǐ	216	语言	yǔyán	247	学校	xuéxiào
186	老	lǎo	217	告诉	gàosu	248	日	rì
187	头	tóu	218	只有	zhǐyǒu	249	多少	duōshǎo
188	这种	zhèzhǒng	219	晚上	wǎnshang	250	可能	kěnéng
189	很多	hěnduō	220	已	yǐ	251	虽然	suīrán
190	道	dào	221	儿子	érzi	252	这里	zhèli
191	条	tiáo	222	高兴	gāoxìng	253	高	gāo
192	同学	tóngxué	223	家里	jiāli	254	只是	zhǐshì
193	许多	xǔduō	224	张	zhāng	255	放	fàng
194	爱	ài	225	不能	bùnéng	256	眼睛	yǎnjing
195	一些	yìxiē	226	看到	kàndào	257	有的	yǒude
196	这么	zhème	227	正	zhèng	258	应该	yīnggāi
197	汉语	hànyǔ	228	花	huā	259	不过	bùguò
198	开始	kāishǐ	229	呀	ya	260	讲	jiǎng
199	所	suǒ	230	后来	hòulái	261	发现	fāxiàn
200	而且	érqiě	231	二	èr	262	句	jù
201	回来	huílái	232	为什么	wèishénme	263	刚	gāng

频度	词语	拼音	频度	词语	拼音	频度	词语	拼音
264	心里	xīnli	294	五	wǔ	323	每	měi
265	穿	chuān	295	常常	chángcháng	324	然而	rán'ér
266	连	lián	296	如	rú	325	甲	jiǎ
267	远	yuǎn	297	少	shǎo	326	些	xiē
268	怎么样	zěnmeyàng			shào	327	希望	xīwàng
269	当然	dāngrán	298	一边	yìbiān	328	说话	shuōhuà
270	电话	diànhuà	299	于	yú	329	参加	cānjiā
271	一天	yìtiān	300	忽然	hūrán	330	第二	dì'èr
272	每天	měitiān	301	行	háng	331	女儿	nǚ'ér
273	哪	nǎ			xíng	332	原来	yuánlái
274	咱们	zánmen	302	一直	yìzhí	333	菜	cài
275	倒	dǎo	303	别人	biérén	334	口	kǒu
		dào	304	然后	ránhòu	335	需要	xūyào
276	么	me	305	或者	huòzhě	336	出去	chūqù
277	哪儿	nǎr	306	衣服	yīfu	337	信	xìn
278	怕	pà	307	分	fēn	338	座	zuò
279	感到	gǎndào	308	该	gāi	339	身体	shēntǐ
280	早	zǎo	309	那个	nàge	340	自然	zìrán
281	妻子	qīzi	310	特别	tèbié	341	唱	chàng
282	往	wǎng	311	文化	wénhuà	342	好像	hǎoxiàng
283	不同	bùtóng	312	极	jí	343	一般	yìbān
284	谢谢	xièxie	313	女人	nǚrén	344	干	gān
285	有人	yǒurén	314	社会	shèhuì			gàn
286	声	shēng	315	终于	zhōngyú	345	妈	mā
287	半	bàn	316	不要	bùyào	346	十分	shífēn
288	人类	rénlèi	317	姑娘	gūniang	347	比较	bǐjiào
289	本	běn	318	全	quán	348	意思	yìsi
290	下来	xiàlái	319	常	cháng	349	越	yuè
291	总	zǒng	320	国家	guójiā	350	红	hóng
292	历史	lìshǐ	321	认为	rènwéi	351	啦	la
293	明天	míngtiān	322	之后	zhīhòu	352	想到	xiǎngdào

频度	词语	拼音	频度	词语	拼音	频度	词语	拼音
353	十	shí	384	不少	bùshǎo	414	一切	yīqiè
354	重要	zhòngyào	385	酒	jiǔ	415	敢	gǎn
355	公司	gōngsī	386	睡	shuì	416	来到	láidào
356	老人	lǎorén	387	心	xīn	417	谈	tán
357	一会儿	yīhuìr	388	名	míng	418	小时	xiǎoshí
358	不好	bùhǎo	389	研究	yánjiū	419	以前	yǐqián
359	下午	xiàwǔ	390	片	piàn	420	点儿	diǎnr
360	一点	yīdiǎn	391	事情	shìqing	421	那里	nàli
361	正在	zhèngzài	392	样子	yàngzi	422	懂	dǒng
362	边	biān	393	脸	liǎn	423	当时	dāngshí
363	家庭	jiātíng	394	情况	qíngkuàng	424	间	jiān
364	认识	rènshi	395	望	wàng	425	名字	míngzi
365	声音	shēngyīn	396	无	wú	426	老爷	lǎoye
366	总是	zǒngshì	397	小姐	xiǎojiě	427	教	jiāo
367	变	biàn	398	八	bā			jiào
368	动物	dòngwù	399	突然	tūrán	428	其	qí
369	号	hào	400	也许	yěxǔ	429	生命	shēngmìng
370	听说	tīngshuō	401	这时	zhèshí	430	路	lù
371	由	yóu	402	大学	dàxué	431	停	tíng
372	最后	zuìhòu	403	算	suàn	432	教授	jiàoshòu
373	发展	fāzhǎn	404	越来越	yuèláiyuè	433	白	bái
374	同	tóng	405	病	bìng	434	不错	bùcuò
375	则	zé	406	回家	huíjiā	435	故事	gùshi
376	准备	zhǔnbèi	407	那儿	nàr	436	漂亮	piàoliang
377	米	mǐ	408	难	nán	437	成为	chéngwéi
378	跳	tiào			nàn	438	离开	líkāi
379	因此	yīncǐ	409	汽车	qìchē	439	满	mǎn
380	读	dú	410	似的	shìde	440	你好	nǐhǎo
381	似乎	sìhū	411	音乐	yīnyuè	441	父母	fùmǔ
382	它们	tāmen	412	真是	zhēnshì	442	美	měi
383	下去	xiàqù	413	卖	mài	443	只要	zhǐyào

频度	词语	拼音	频度	词语	拼音	频度	词语	拼音
444	帮	bāng	474	受	shòu	505	打开	dǎkāi
445	黑	hēi	475	外	wài	506	大概	dàgài
446	换	huàn	476	别的	biéde	507	动	dòng
447	经过	jīngguò	477	除了	chúle	508	房子	fángzi
448	生	shēng	478	得到	dédào	509	飞	fēi
449	由于	yóuyú	479	回到	huídào	510	寄	jì
450	丈夫	zhàngfu	480	结婚	jiéhūn	511	爬	pá
451	美丽	měilì	481	精神	jīngshen	512	有点	yǒudiǎn
452	那些	nàxiē	482	明白	míngbai	513	关系	guānxi
453	药	yào	483	女	nǚ	514	了解	liǎojiě
454	一点儿	yīdiǎnr	484	哭	kū	515	那样	nàyàng
455	以为	yǐwéi	485	气	qì	516	茶	chá
456	只好	zhǐhǎo	486	姓	xìng	517	各种	gèzhǒng
457	城市	chéngshì	487	眼	yǎn	518	马上	mǎshàng
458	回答	huídá	488	鱼	yú	519	要是	yàoshì
459	艺术	yìshù	489	慢慢	mànmàn	520	不知	bùzhī
460	饭	fàn	490	生日	shēngrì	521	人民	rénmín
461	拉	lā	491	幸福	xìngfú	522	听到	tīngdào
462	七	qī	492	永远	yǒngyuǎn	523	影响	yǐngxiǎng
463	元	yuán	493	愿意	yuànyì	524	有时	yǒushí
464	吃饭	chīfàn	494	方面	fāngmiàn	525	注意	zhùyì
465	发	fā	495	曾	céng	526	步	bù
		fà	496	过来	guòlái	527	另	lìng
466	决定	juédìng	497	容易	róngyì	528	挺	tǐng
467	课	kè	498	支	zhī	529	按	àn
468	选择	xuǎnzé	499	表示	biǎoshì	530	办	bàn
469	不会	bùhuì	500	进行	jìnxíng	531	包	bāo
470	对于	duìyú	501	经常	jīngcháng	532	掉	diào
471	房间	fángjiān	502	其实	qíshí	533	请问	qǐngwèn
472	介绍	jièshào	503	忘	wàng	534	仍然	réngrán
473	山	shān	504	错	cuò	535	宿舍	sùshè

频度	词语	拼音	频度	词语	拼音	频度	词语	拼音
536	昨天	zuótiān	566	仿佛	fǎngfú	597	环境	huánjìng
537	场	cháng	567	放在	fàngzài	598	离	lí
		chǎng	568	活动	huódòng	599	礼物	lǐwù
538	二十	èrshí	569	上课	shàngkè	600	路上	lùshang
539	发生	fāshēng	570	玩	wán	601	内	nèi
540	感觉	gǎnjué	571	找到	zhǎodào	602	清楚	qīngchu
541	还要	háiyào	572	成功	chénggōng	603	身上	shēnshang
542	技术	jìshù	573	出现	chūxiàn	604	售货员	shòuhuòyuán
543	辆	liàng	574	里面	lǐmiàn	605	中文	zhōngwén
544	人家	rénjia	575	实在	shízài	606	变成	biànchéng
545	甚至	shènzhì	576	碗	wǎn	607	不仅	bùjǐn
546	不但	bùdàn	577	洗	xǐ	608	大约	dàyuē
547	努力	nǔlì	578	颜色	yánsè	609	九	jiǔ
548	太阳	tàiyáng	579	变化	biànhuà	610	来说	láishuō
549	船	chuán	580	春天	chūntiān	611	脸上	liǎnshang
550	热	rè	581	靠	kào	612	万	wàn
551	完全	wánquán	582	哪里	nǎli	613	要求	yāoqiú
552	段	duàn	583	这次	zhècì	614	意义	yìyì
553	服务员	fúwùyuán	584	健康	jiànkāng	615	表现	biǎoxiàn
554	既	jì	585	今年	jīnnián	616	分钟	fēnzhōng
555	所有	suǒyǒu	586	竟	jìng	617	很快	hěnkuài
556	爷爷	yéye	587	六	liù	618	脚	jiǎo
557	作为	zuòwéi	588	能够	nénggòu	619	结果	jiéguǒ
558	接着	jiēzhe	589	人口	rénkǒu	620	深	shēn
559	习惯	xíguàn	590	套	tào	621	玩儿	wánr
560	比赛	bǐsài	591	帮助	bāngzhù	622	往往	wǎngwǎng
561	风	fēng	592	对不起	duìbuqǐ	623	接	jiē
562	哦	ò	593	胡同	hútòng	624	其他	qítā
563	认真	rènzhēn	594	文字	wénzì	625	日子	rìzi
564	太太	tàitai	595	抱	bào	626	手里	shǒuli
565	医生	yīshēng	596	笔	bǐ	627	天气	tiānqì

113

频度	词语	拼音	频度	词语	拼音	频度	词语	拼音
628	知识	zhīshi	659	直	zhí	689	照	zhào
629	自行车	zìxíngchē	660	必须	bìxū	690	打算	dǎsuan
630	感情	gǎnqíng	661	产生	chǎnshēng	691	欢迎	huānyíng
631	挂	guà	662	面	miàn	692	门口	ménkǒu
632	旅行	lǚxíng	663	同时	tóngshí	693	取	qǔ
633	清	qīng	664	休息	xiūxi	694	相信	xiāngxìn
634	首先	shǒuxiān	665	有名	yǒumíng	695	怎样	zěnyàng
635	早上	zǎoshang	666	重	zhòng	696	罢	bà
636	装	zhuāng	667	低	dī	697	冬天	dōngtiān
637	丰富	fēngfù	668	多么	duōme	698	机会	jīhuì
638	进来	jìnlái	669	借	jiè	699	渐渐	jiànjiàn
639	落	luò	670	斤	jīn	700	就要	jiùyào
640	民族	mínzú	671	进去	jìnqù	701	面前	miànqián
641	年轻	niánqīng	672	客人	kèrén	702	破	pò
642	农民	nóngmín	673	快乐	kuàilè	703	提	tí
643	现代	xiàndài	674	困难	kùnnan	704	毕业	bìyè
644	一家	yījiā	675	楼	lóu	705	管	guǎn
645	自	zì	676	猫	māo	706	教室	jiàoshì
646	办法	bànfǎ	677	那时	nàshí	707	骑	qí
647	各	gè	678	司机	sījī	708	受到	shòudào
648	即使	jíshǐ	679	腿	tuǐ	709	替	tì
649	那天	nàtiān	680	转	zhuǎn	710	遇到	yùdào
650	牛	niú			zhuàn	711	之间	zhījiān
651	兴趣	xìngqù	681	作	zuò	712	非	fēi
652	比如	bǐrú	682	床	chuáng	713	根	gēn
653	遍	biàn	683	封	fēng	714	坏	huài
654	地球	dìqiú	684	工人	gōngrén	715	几乎	jīhū
655	光	guāng	685	活	huó	716	嫁	jià
656	喊	hǎn	686	冷	lěng	717	紧张	jǐnzhāng
657	记	jì	687	医院	yīyuàn	718	旧	jiù
658	流	liú	688	有时候	yǒushíhou	719	弄	nòng

频度	词语	拼音	频度	词语	拼音	频度	词语	拼音
720	世纪	shìjì	751	方式	fāngshì	782	数	shǔ
721	听见	tīngjiàn	752	她们	tāmen			shù
722	小伙子	xiǎohuǒzi	753	狼	láng	783	眼泪	yǎnlèi
723	并且	bìngqiě	754	绿色	lǜsè	784	一面	yīmiàn
724	不断	bùduàn	755	贴	tiē	785	英语	yīngyǔ
725	聪明	cōngming	756	原因	yuányīn	786	有意思	yǒuyìsi
726	海洋	hǎiyáng	757	主人	zhǔrén	787	办公室	bàngōngshì
727	挤	jǐ	758	最近	zuìjìn	788	长大	zhǎngdà
728	记得	jìde	759	作品	zuòpǐn	789	弟弟	dìdi
729	京剧	jīngjù	760	词	cí	790	更加	gèngjiā
730	留	liú	761	干什么	gànshénme	791	公园	gōngyuán
731	旁边	pángbiān	762	经理	jīnglǐ	792	互相	hùxiāng
732	陪	péi	763	考虑	kǎolǜ	793	简直	jiǎnzhí
733	如此	rúcǐ	764	留下	liúxià	794	马	mǎ
734	响	xiǎng	765	水平	shuǐpíng	795	肉	ròu
735	真正	zhēnzhèng	766	通过	tōngguò	796	生产	shēngchǎn
736	本来	běnlái	767	图书馆	túshūguǎn	797	思想	sīxiǎng
737	差不多	chàbuduō	768	屋子	wūzi	798	一下子	yīxiàzi
738	朝	cháo	769	纸	zhǐ	799	照片	zhàopiàn
739	从此	cóngcǐ	770	爸	bà	800	病人	bìngrén
740	大夫	dàifu	771	班	bān	801	不久	bùjiǔ
741	电脑	diànnǎo	772	不见	bùjiàn	802	参观	cānguān
742	赶	gǎn	773	第三	dìsān	803	处	chǔ
743	哥哥	gēge	774	青年	qīngnián			chù
744	简单	jiǎndān	775	直到	zhídào	804	地上	dìshang
745	立刻	lìkè	776	飞机	fēijī	805	地震	dìzhèn
746	说道	shuōdào	777	够	gòu	806	电视	diànshì
747	因	yīn	778	考试	kǎoshì	807	电影	diànyǐng
748	只能	zhǐnéng	779	骂	mà	808	方法	fāngfǎ
749	不可	bùkě	780	使用	shǐyòng	809	感谢	gǎnxiè
750	而是	érshì	781	事业	shìyè	810	狗	gǒu

频度	词语	拼音	频度	词语	拼音	频度	词语	拼音
811	皇帝	huángdì	842	奇怪	qíguài			chà
812	即	jí	843	人生	rénshēng	873	担心	dānxīn
813	急	jí	844	商店	shāngdiàn	874	刚才	gāngcái
814	经济	jīngjì	845	上面	shàngmian	875	回去	huíqù
815	累	lèi	846	上去	shàngqù	876	那位	nàwèi
816	每年	měinián	847	双	shuāng	877	篇	piān
817	某	mǒu	848	特点	tèdiǎn	878	首	shǒu
818	男	nán	849	伟大	wěidà	879	文学	wénxué
819	男人	nánrén	850	喂	wèi	880	杯	bēi
820	任何	rènhé	851	夏天	xiàtiān	881	不行	bùxíng
821	树	shù	852	心中	xīnzhōng	882	带来	dàilái
822	抓	zhuā	853	养	yǎng	883	花园	huāyuán
823	到处	dàochù	854	游	yóu	884	记者	jìzhě
824	搞	gǎo	855	主要	zhǔyào	885	久	jiǔ
825	排	pái	856	不用	bùyòng	886	能力	nénglì
826	其中	qízhōng	857	此	cǐ	887	生气	shēngqì
827	想起	xiǎngqǐ	858	放心	fàngxīn	888	文章	wénzhāng
828	者	zhě	859	关心	guānxīn	889	显得	xiǎnde
829	嘴	zuǐ	860	考	kǎo	890	读书	dúshū
830	唉	āi	861	邻居	línjū	891	方便	fāngbiàn
831	传统	chuántǒng	862	热情	rèqíng	892	河	hé
832	等等	děngděng	863	如何	rúhé	893	经验	jīngyàn
833	幅	fú	864	时代	shídài	894	筷子	kuàizi
834	副	fù	865	态度	tàidù	895	票	piào
835	古代	gǔdài	866	提高	tígāo	896	身	shēn
836	回头	huítóu	867	一句话	yījùhuà	897	十几	shíjǐ
837	继续	jìxù	868	著名	zhùmíng	898	市场	shìchǎng
838	结束	jiéshù	869	着急	zháojí	899	消息	xiāoxi
839	尽	jìn	870	搬	bān	900	心理	xīnlǐ
840	看来	kànlái	871	不管	bùguǎn	901	夜	yè
841	每个	měigè	872	差	chā	902	雨	yǔ

116

频度	词语	拼音	频度	词语	拼音	频度	词语	拼音
903	预报	yùbào	934	存在	cúnzài	964	锻炼	duànliàn
904	植物	zhíwù	935	根据	gēnjù	965	饿	è
905	只见	zhǐjiàn	936	画家	huàjiā	966	汉字	hànzì
906	桌子	zhuōzi	937	苦	kǔ	967	鸡	jī
907	歌	gē	938	老虎	lǎohǔ	968	剪	jiǎn
908	贵	guì	939	妹妹	mèimei	969	教育	jiàoyù
909	国际	guójì	940	舒服	shūfu	970	解决	jiějué
910	火	huǒ	941	提出	tíchū	971	具有	jùyǒu
911	节目	jiémù	942	寻	xún	972	盘	pán
912	近	jìn	943	演员	yǎnyuán	973	如今	rújīn
913	俩	liǎ	944	有点儿	yǒudiǎnr	974	疼	téng
914	留学生	liúxuésheng	945	再见	zàijiàn	975	天天	tiāntiān
915	奶奶	nǎinai	946	份	fèn	976	同意	tóngyì
916	派	pài	947	公共	gōnggòng	977	引起	yǐnqǐ
917	群众	qúnzhòng	948	过程	guòchéng	978	有关	yǒuguān
918	晚	wǎn	949	空	kōng	979	足球	zúqiú
919	无论	wúlùn			kòng	980	报	bào
920	指	zhǐ				981	擦	cā
921	中间	zhōngjiān	950	嘛	ma	982	充满	chōngmǎn
922	代表	dàibiǎo	951	十二	shí'èr	983	吹	chuī
923	到底	dàodǐ	952	收	shōu	984	定	dìng
924	关	guān	953	叔叔	shūshu	985	感动	gǎndòng
925	见面	jiànmiàn	954	抬	tái	986	婚姻	hūnyīn
926	饺子	jiǎozi	955	天空	tiānkōng	987	假	jiǎ
927	绿	lù	956	心情	xīnqíng			jià
928	那种	nàzhǒng	957	烟	yān	988	坚持	jiānchí
929	女孩	nǚhái	958	园林	yuánlín	989	进入	jìnrù
930	入	rù	959	至于	zhìyú	990	颗	kē
931	上午	shàngwǔ	960	保护	bǎohù	991	念	niàn
932	以及	yǐjí	961	不如	bùrú	992	躺	tǎng
933	摆	bǎi	962	层	céng	993	学会	xuéhuì
			963	成绩	chéngjì			

118

频度	词语	拼音	频度	词语	拼音	频度	词语	拼音
994	专家	zhuānjiā	1025	改变	gǎibiàn	1055	伤	shāng
995	不再	bùzài	1026	经历	jīnglì	1056	少爷	shàoye
996	从前	cóngqián	1027	客气	kèqi	1057	杂志	zázhì
997	妇女	fùnǚ	1028	肯定	kěndìng	1058	曾经	céngjīng
998	跟着	gēnzhe	1029	理解	lǐjiě	1059	之中	zhīzhōng
999	好吃	hǎochī	1030	立	lì	1060	左右	zuǒyòu
1000	好多	hǎoduō	1031	亮	liàng	1061	表达	biǎodá
1001	科学	kēxué	1032	农村	nóngcūn	1062	冲	chōng
1002	失去	shīqù	1033	上来	shànglái	1063	创造	chuàngzào
1003	外国	wàiguó	1034	虽	suī	1064	从来	cónglái
1004	外面	wàimiàn	1035	下班	xiàbān	1065	待	dài
1005	一百	yībǎi	1036	箱子	xiāngzi	1066	感	gǎn
1006	正是	zhèngshì	1037	星期	xīngqī	1067	好好儿	hǎohāor
1007	至	zhì	1038	一块	yīkuài	1068	黄	huáng
1008	组合	zǔhé	1039	一生	yīshēng	1069	年纪	niánjì
1009	作家	zuòjiā	1040	以上	yǐshàng	1070	年轻人	niánqīngrén
1010	包括	bāokuò	1041	月亮	yuèliang	1071	商量	shāngliang
1011	夫人	fūrén	1042	安排	ānpái	1072	师傅	shīfu
1012	将来	jiānglái	1043	背	bēi	1073	时期	shíqī
1013	姐姐	jiějie			bèi	1074	微笑	wēixiào
1014	举行	jǔxíng	1044	不够	bùgòu	1075	象征	xiàngzhēng
1015	另外	lìngwài	1045	打电话	dǎdiànhuà	1076	一眼	yīyǎn
1016	年代	niándài	1046	发出	fāchū	1077	印象	yìnxiàng
1017	鸟	niǎo	1047	建筑	jiànzhù	1078	约	yuē
1018	热闹	rènao	1048	尽管	jǐnguǎn	1079	运动	yùndòng
1019	送给	sònggěi	1049	空气	kōngqì	1080	主意	zhǔyi
1020	晚饭	wǎnfàn	1050	理想	lǐxiǎng	1081	便宜	piányi
1021	屋里	wūli	1051	令	lìng	1082	道理	dàolǐ
1022	无法	wúfǎ	1052	满意	mǎnyì	1083	耳朵	ěrduo
1023	一时	yīshí	1053	毛	máo	1084	根本	gēnběn
1024	这时候	zhèshíhou	1054	闹	nào	1085	果然	guǒrán

频度	词语	拼音	频度	词语	拼音	频度	词语	拼音
1086	价值	jiàzhí	1117	觉	jiào	1146	五十	wǔshí
					jué	1147	以外	yǐwài
1087	接受	jiēshòu	1118	恐怕	kǒngpà	1148	便是	biànshì
1088	科学家	kēxuéjiā	1119	练习	liànxí	1149	表演	biǎoyǎn
1089	棵	kē	1120	拍	pāi	1150	刚刚	gānggāng
1090	可爱	kě'ài	1121	强	qiáng	1151	个人	gèrén
1091	蓝	lán	1122	三十	sānshí	1152	好看	hǎokàn
1092	每次	měicì	1123	上学	shàngxué	1153	合适	héshì
1093	骑车	qíchē	1124	选	xuǎn	1154	哼	hēng
1094	前面	qiánmian	1125	有趣	yǒuqù	1155	火车	huǒchē
1095	去年	qùnián	1126	周围	zhōuwéi	1156	夹	jiā
1096	全国	quánguó	1127	祝	zhù	1157	领导	lǐngdǎo
1097	确实	quèshí	1128	自由	zìyóu	1158	慢	màn
1098	仍	réng	1129	组织	zǔzhī	1159	内容	nèiróng
1099	随着	suízhe	1130	辫子	biànzi	1160	您好	nínhǎo
1100	甜	tián	1131	布	bù	1161	穷	qióng
1101	头发	tóufa	1132	草	cǎo	1162	全部	quánbù
1102	我家	wǒjiā	1133	草原	cǎoyuán	1163	群	qún
1103	下面	xiàmian	1134	戴	dài	1164	若	ruò
1104	尤其	yóuqí	1135	分析	fēnxī	1165	身边	shēnbiān
1105	怎么办	zěnmebàn	1136	号码	hàomǎ	1166	诗	shī
1106	仔细	zǐxì	1137	究竟	jiūjìng	1167	石头	shítou
1107	部	bù	1138	据说	jùshuō	1168	天上	tiānshàng
1108	猜	cāi	1139	乱	luàn	1169	完成	wánchéng
1109	大声	dàshēng	1140	难道	nándào	1170	咬	yǎo
1110	第二天	dì'èrtiān	1141	普通	pǔtōng	1171	一共	yīgòng
1111	堆	duī	1142	散	sǎn	1172	早晨	zǎochen
1112	房	fáng			sàn	1173	值得	zhídé
1113	革命	gémìng				1174	众	zhòng
1114	后面	hòumian	1143	生存	shēngcún	1175	周末	zhōumò
1115	见到	jiàndào	1144	所谓	suǒwèi	1176	作用	zuòyòng
1116	交	jiāo	1145	趟	tàng			

频度	词语	拼音	频度	词语	拼音	频度	词语	拼音
1177	表	biǎo	1208	千	qiān	1239	平时	píngshí
1178	从小	cóngxiǎo	1209	山上	shānshang	1240	人员	rényuán
1179	灯	dēng	1210	蛇	shé	1241	森林	sēnlín
1180	丢	diū	1211	狮子	shīzi	1242	叔	shū
1181	断	duàn	1212	蔬菜	shūcài	1243	数学	shùxué
1182	顿	dùn	1213	睡觉	shuìjiào	1244	吐	tǔ
1183	红色	hóngsè	1214	危险	wēixiǎn			tù
1184	获得	huòdé	1215	文	wén	1245	小时候	xiǎoshíhou
1185	加	jiā	1216	吸引	xīyǐn	1246	意见	yìjiàn
1186	可惜	kěxī	1217	相当	xiāngdāng	1247	语法	yǔfǎ
1187	类	lèi	1218	愉快	yúkuài	1248	早已	zǎoyǐ
1188	麻烦	máfan	1219	之前	zhīqián	1249	整个	zhěnggè
1189	桥	qiáo	1220	治	zhì	1250	之一	zhīyī
1190	书店	shūdiàn	1221	祖国	zǔguó	1251	职员	zhíyuán
1191	同志	tóngzhì	1222	春节	chūnjié	1252	子	zǐ
1192	偷	tōu	1223	呆	dāi	1253	补	bǔ
1193	现象	xiànxiàng	1224	地区	dìqū	1254	不好意思	bùhǎoyìsi
1194	香	xiāng	1225	东	dōng	1255	答应	dāyìng
1195	性格	xìnggé	1226	肚子	dùzi	1256	的话	dehuà
1196	一阵	yīzhèn	1227	反对	fǎnduì	1257	懂得	dǒngde
1197	银行	yínháng	1228	关于	guānyú	1258	翻译	fānyì
1198	撞	zhuàng	1229	花儿	huār	1259	附近	fùjìn
1199	组	zǔ	1230	家乡	jiāxiāng	1260	工厂	gōngchǎng
1200	单位	dānwèi	1231	讲究	jiǎngjiū	1261	观念	guānniàn
1201	和尚	héshang	1232	解释	jiěshì	1262	湖	hú
1202	荷花	héhuā	1233	开玩笑	kāiwánxiào	1263	街上	jiēshang
1203	进步	jìnbù	1234	哩	li	1264	居然	jūrán
1204	肯	kěn	1235	连忙	liánmáng	1265	例如	lìrú
1205	旅游	lǚyóu	1236	联系	liánxì	1266	女性	nǚxìng
1206	满足	mǎnzú	1237	练	liàn	1267	情绪	qíngxù
1207	气氛	qìfēn	1238	嗯	èng	1268	球	qiú

频度	词语	拼音	频度	词语	拼音	频度	词语	拼音
1269	撒	sā	1299	水果	shuǐguǒ	1329	角	jiǎo
1270	绳	shéng	1300	题	tí	1330	摸	mō
1271	摔	shuāi	1301	痛苦	tòngkǔ	1331	婆婆	pópo
1272	说完	shuōwán	1302	忘记	wàngjì	1332	事物	shìwù
1273	条件	tiáojiàn	1303	吓	xià	1333	瘦	shòu
1274	西	xī	1304	鲜花	xiānhuā	1334	说明	shuōmíng
1275	西方	xīfāng	1305	行为	xíngwéi	1335	四十	sìshí
1276	相	xiāng	1306	雪	xuě	1336	太祖母	tàizǔmǔ
		xiàng	1307	眼前	yǎnqián	1337	谈话	tánhuà
1277	小心	xiǎoxīn	1308	摇	yáo	1338	通	tōng
1278	星期六	xīngqīliù	1309	依然	yīrán	1339	同样	tóngyàng
1279	一半	yībàn	1310	应	yīng	1340	推	tuī
1280	在家	zàijiā			yìng	1341	校园	xiàoyuán
1281	早就	zǎojiù	1311	愿	yuàn	1342	修	xiū
1282	照顾	zhàogù	1312	中午	zhōngwǔ	1343	圆	yuán
1283	中医	zhōngyī	1313	中心	zhōngxīn	1344	增加	zēngjiā
1284	捉	zhuō	1314	追	zhuī	1345	掌柜	zhǎngguì
1285	称	chēng	1315	最好	zuìhǎo	1346	知	zhī
1286	短	duǎn	1316	半天	bàntiān	1347	资料	zīliào
1287	改	gǎi	1317	不必	bùbì	1348	爱情	àiqíng
1288	广告	guǎnggào	1318	出发	chūfā	1349	安静	ānjìng
1289	恨	hèn	1319	错误	cuòwù	1350	反正	fǎnzhèng
1290	较	jiào	1320	达到	dádào	1351	方	fāng
1291	口袋	kǒudai	1321	顶	dǐng	1352	付	fù
1292	去世	qùshì	1322	各地	gèdì	1353	鬼	guǐ
1293	热烈	rèliè	1323	怪	guài	1354	好几	hǎojǐ
1294	人物	rénwù	1324	观察	guānchá	1355	加上	jiāshàng
1295	上班	shàngbān	1325	国	guó	1356	姐	jiě
1296	神	shén	1326	合	hé	1357	可怜	kělián
1297	始终	shǐzhōng	1327	及	jí	1358	没关系	méiguānxi
1298	是否	shìfǒu	1328	计划	jìhuà	1359	命	mìng

频度	词语	拼音	频度	词语	拼音	频度	词语	拼音
1360	哪个	nǎge	1391	新年	xīnnián	1422	营业员	yíngyèyuán
1361	球迷	qiúmí	1392	学问	xuéwen	1423	邮局	yóujú
1362	劝	quàn	1393	一辈子	yībèizi	1424	云	yún
1363	扔	rēng	1394	英文	yīngwén	1425	责任	zérèn
1364	婶	shěn	1395	语汇	yǔhuì	1426	占	zhàn
1365	兴奋	xīngfèn	1396	掌握	zhǎngwò	1427	主任	zhǔrèn
1366	羊	yáng	1397	坐下	zuòxià	1428	嘴里	zuǐli
1367	夜里	yèli	1398	查	chá	1429	安慰	ānwèi
1368	友好	yǒuhǎo	1399	城里	chéngli	1430	表情	biǎoqíng
1369	院子	yuànzi	1400	传说	chuánshuō	1431	不安	bù'ān
1370	煮	zhǔ	1401	大量	dàliàng	1432	部分	bùfen
1371	出生	chūshēng	1402	队	duì	1433	厨房	chúfáng
1372	大海	dàhǎi	1403	盖	gài	1434	大门	dàmén
1373	代	dài	1404	几十	jǐshí	1435	低声	dīshēng
1374	得意	déyì	1405	既然	jìrán	1436	店	diàn
1375	端	duān	1406	家中	jiāzhōng	1437	放弃	fàngqì
1376	翻	fān	1407	惊	jīng	1438	复杂	fùzá
1377	饭店	fàndiàn	1408	老太太	lǎotàitai	1439	工具	gōngjù
1378	方向	fāngxiàng	1409	露	lù	1440	公里	gōnglǐ
1379	构成	gòuchéng	1410	年龄	niánlíng	1441	故意	gùyì
1380	猴子	hóuzi	1411	平静	píngjìng	1442	官	guān
1381	激动	jīdòng	1412	千万	qiānwàn	1443	建立	jiànlì
1382	老板	lǎobǎn	1413	试	shì	1444	力气	lìqi
1383	泪	lèi	1414	味道	wèidào	1445	脸色	liǎnsè
1384	利用	lìyòng	1415	享受	xiǎngshòu	1446	目的	mùdì
1385	聊	liáo	1416	想象	xiǎngxiàng	1447	男孩	nánhái
1386	胖	pàng	1417	消失	xiāoshī	1448	苹果	píngguǒ
1387	墙上	qiángshang	1418	形态	xíngtài	1449	求	qiú
1388	随便	suíbiàn	1419	一年	yīnián	1450	身子	shēnzi
1389	提供	tígōng	1420	乙	yǐ	1451	士兵	shìbīng
1390	未	wèi	1421	应当	yīngdāng	1452	收拾	shōushi

频度	词语	拼音	频度	词语	拼音	频度	词语	拼音
1453	叹	tàn	1469	婚礼	hūnlǐ	1485	挑	tiāo
1454	文明	wénmíng	1470	建议	jiànyì	1486	透	tòu
1455	我国	wǒguó	1471	紧	jǐn	1487	相同	xiāngtóng
1456	现实	xiànshí	1472	镜子	jìngzi	1488	笑话	xiàohua
1457	谢	xiè	1473	巨大	jùdà	1489	形象	xíngxiàng
1458	新鲜	xīnxiān	1474	据	jù	1490	阳光	yángguāng
1459	一部分	yībùfen	1475	劳动	láodòng	1491	游戏	yóuxì
1460	一口气	yīkǒuqì	1476	冒	mào	1492	政治	zhèngzhì
1461	樱花	yīnghuā	1477	美好	měihǎo	1493	众人	zhòngrén
1462	造成	zàochéng	1478	碰	pèng	1494	竹子	zhúzi
1463	正好	zhènghǎo	1479	全家	quánjiā	1495	白天	báitiān
1464	准	zhǔn	1480	少年	shàonián	1496	标准	biāozhǔn
1465	不得不	bùdébù	1481	实际上	shíjìshang	1497	从不	cóngbù
1466	材料	cáiliào	1482	试试	shìshì	1498	从而	cóng'ér
1467	产品	chǎnpǐn	1483	收入	shōurù	1499	对象	duìxiàng
1468	反映	fǎnyìng	1484	台	tái	1500	赶紧	gǎnjǐn

123

(引自："中国语言生活状况报告"课题组. 中国语言生活状况报告 (2006). 北京：商务印书馆，2007)

参考资料

中国国家汉语国际推广领导小组办公室.国际汉语教师标准.北京: 外语教学与研究出版社，2007.

The Office of Chinese Language Council International. *Standards for Teachers of Chinese to Speakers of Other Languages*, Beijing: Foreign Language Teaching and Research Press.2007.

中国国家汉语国际推广领导小组办公室．国际汉语能力标准．北京：外语教学与研究出版社，2007.

The Office of Chinese Language Council International. *Chinese Language Proficiency Scales for Speakers of Other Languages*, Beijing: Foreign Language Teaching and Research Press.2007.

中华人民共和国教育部．普通高中英语课程标准（实验）．北京：人民教育出版社，2003.

Board of Education. Commonwealth of Virginia (Ed.). *Foreign Language Standards of Learning for Virginia Public Schools*. Richmond, VA. USA. 2007.

California Department of Education (Ed.). *Foreign Language Framework for California Public Schools: Kindergarten Through Grade Twelve*. Sacramento, CA. USA. 2003.

College Board. *Chinese Language and Culture—Course Description—Audio Files:* The College Board. USA. 2007.

Kansas Committee for International Education in the Schools. *Report of the Kansas Task Force on Chinese Language Training*. Kansas. USA. 2006.

Kean, J., Grady, S., & Sandrock, P. *Wisconsin's Model Academic Standards for Foreign Languages,* USA. 1997. Available from http://dpi.wi.gov/standards/pdf/fl.pdf

Massachusetts Department Education. *Massachusetts Foreign Languages Curriculum Framework*. Journal. USA. 1999. Retrieved from http://www.doe.mass.edu/frameworks/foreign/1999.pdf

Minnesota Department of Education. *Chinese Language Programs Curriculum Development Project*. Roseville, MN: Minnesota Department of Education. USA. 2007.

State of New Jersey. Department of Education. *New Jersey World Languages Curriculum Framework, USA*. 1999. Available from http://www.nj.gov/education/frameworks/worldlanguages/

Victorian Curriculum and Assessment Authority. *Chinese, Second Language, Second Language Advanced*. In R. Learner (Eds.), USA. 2004. Available from http://www.vcaa.vic.edu.au/vce/studies/lote/chinese2nd/ChineseSLASD.pdf

Ministère de l'éducation nationale (dir. Alain Weinich), *Programme des Langues Etrangères et Régionales à l'Ecole primaire Chinois*. Bulletin officiel de l'éducation nationale n°4 hors-série, Paris, France, 29 août 2002.

Ministère de l'éducation nationale (dir. Isabelle Pillet), *Programme des Collèges Langues Vivantes Etrangères au Palier I Chinois.* Bulletin officiel de l'éducation nationale n°6 hors-série, Paris, France, 25 août 2005

Ministère de l'éducation nationale (dir. Joël Bellassen), *Programmes des Lycées Chinois Classe de Seconde générale et Technologique.* Bulletin officiel de l'éducation nationale n°7 hors-série, Paris, France, 3 octobre 2002

Ministère de l'éducation nationale (dir. Joël Bellassen), *Programmes des Lycées Chinois Classe Terminal-Séries Générales et Technologiques.* Bulletin officiel de l'éducation nationale n°5 hors-série, Paris, France, 9 septembre. 2004.

Bayerisches Staatsministerium für Unterricht und Kultus. *Lehrplan für Chinesisch als spätbeginnende Fremdsprache.* [Z] KWMBl (Das Amtsblatt der Bayerischen Staatsministerien für Unterricht und Kultus und Wissenschaft, Forschung und Kunst) I So.-Nr. 4/1995, S. 86-117. http://www.isb.bayern.de/isb/download.aspx?DownloadFileID=b82ca 4a509a417778d255d7c9c6b9369

Ministerium für Kultus, Jugend und Sport Baden-Württemberg (Hrsg., in Zusammenarbeit mit dem Landesinstitut für Erziehung und Unterricht Stuttgart). *Bildungsplan 2004. Allgemein bildendes Gymnasium.* [Z] Stuttgart, 2004, S. 510-514. http://www.bildung-staerkt-menschen.de/service/ downloads/Bildungsplaene/Gymnasium/Gymnasium_Bildungsplan_Gesamt.pdf

Senatsverwaltung für Bildung, Jugend und Sport Berlin (Hrsg.). *Rahmenlehrplan für die gymnasiale Oberstufe. Chinesisch.* [Z] Berlin. 2006. http://www.berlin.de/imperia/md/ content/sen-bildung/schulorganisation/lehrplaene/sek2_chinesisch.pdf

Senator für Bildung und Wissenschaft Bremen (Hrsg.). *Rahmenplan für die Sekundarstufe II-gymnasiale Oberstufe. Chinesisch als spät beginnende Fremdsprache.* [Z] Bremen.2000. http://lehrplan.bremen.de/sek2a/aufgabenfeld1/chinesisch/rahmenplan/download

Ministry of Education of Thailand. *Basic Education Curriculum B.E. 2544* A.D. Thailand, 2001.

日本中国语教育学会学力基準プロジェクト委員会（古川裕、郭春貴、山田真一、武信彰、與水优）編，中国語初級段階学習指導ガイドライン，东京，日本，中国语教育学会，2007 年 3 月。

（財）国際文化フォーラム（胡兴智、古川裕、千场由美子、森茂岳雄、山田真一、水口景子、藤井达也、植村麻纪子）編，高等学校の中国語と韓国朝鮮語：学習のめやす（試行版），財団法人国際文化フォーラム，2007 年 3 月。

Alberta Education. *Chinese (Mandarin) Language Arts Kindergarten to Grade 12 Call for Resources (Cfr–0501).* Edmonton, AB, 2005. PDF. Alberta Learning. 3 March 2005. <http:// www.education.gov.ab.ca/resources/calls/cfr0501.pdf>.

Alberta. Alberta Education. *Chinese Language and Culture 10-3y, 20-3y*, 30-3y. Edmonton, AB: Alberta Learning, 2005.

Alberta. Alberta Education. *Chinese Language and Culture 10-6y, 20-6y, 30-6y*. Edmonton, AB: Alberta Learning, 2005.

Alberta. Alberta Education. *Chinese Language and Culture Nine-Year Program Grades 4-5*. Interim ed. Edmonton, AB: Alberta Learning, 2006.

Alberta. Alberta Education. *Chinese Language and Culture Six-Year Program Grades 7-8-9*. Edmonton, AB: Alberta Learning, 2005.

Alberta. Alberta Education. *Chinese Language Arts 10-20-30*. Edmonton, AB: Alberta Learning, 2006.

Alberta. Alberta Education. *Chinese Language Arts Kindergarten to Grade 9*. Edmonton, AB: Alberta Learning, 2006.

Alberta. Learning and Teaching Resources Branch. *Chinese Language and Culture, Grades 4–12, Grades 7–9, 10s–20s–30s, 10–20–30, Alberta Authorized Resource List and Annotated Bibliography*. Edmonton, AB: Alberta Learning, 2006.

Alexander, L. G., et al. *English Grammatical Structure: A General Syllabus for Teachers*. London: Longman, 1975.

American Council on the Teaching of Foreign Languages. Standards for Foreign Language Learning: Preparing for the Twenty-First Century. In Robert C. Lafayette and American Council on the Teaching of Foreign Languages. Vols(eds) *National Standards: A Catalyst for Reform*. Lincolnwood, IL: National Textbook Co., 1996. 211-19.

Archibald, John. *Second Language Acquisition (Chapter 14). Contemporary Linguistic Analysis: An Introduction*. Eds. William D. O'Grady and Michael Dobrovolsky. 3rd ed. vols. Toronto, ON: Copp Clark Pitman, 1996. 471-504.

Bachman, Lyle F. *Fundamental Considerations in Language Testing*. Oxford: Oxford University Press, 1990.

Barmé, Geremie R. *In the Red: On Contemporary Chinese Culture*. New York, NY: Columbia University Press, 1999.

Cordasco, Francesco. *Bilingual Education in New York City: A Compendium of Reports*. Bilingual-Bicultural Education in the United States. New York, NY: Arno Press, 1978.

Cordasco, Francesco. *The Bilingual-Bicultural Child and the Question of Intelligence*. Bilingual-Bicultural Education in the United States. New York, NY: Arno Press, 1978.

Cordasco, Francesco. *Bilingualism and the Bilingual Child: Challenges and Problems*. Bilingual-Bicultural Education in the United States. New York, NY: Arno Press, 1978.

Core Knowledge Foundation. *American Literature Syllabus*. PDF. (2002). 9 December, 2002. <http://coreknowledge.org/CK/resrcs/syllabi/PDF/AmericanLitSyllabus.pdf>.

Core Knowledge Foundation. *Art History Syllabus*. PDF. (2002). 9 December 2002. <http://coreknowledge.org/CK/resrcs/syllabi/PDF/ArtHistorySyllabus.pdf>.

Core Knowledge Foundation. *Biology Syllabus*. PDF. (2002). 9 December 2002. <http://coreknowledge.org/CK/resrcs/syllabi/PDF/BiologySyllabus.pdf>.

Core Knowledge Foundation. *British and World Literature Syllabus*. PDF. (2002). 9 December 2002. <http://coreknowledge.org/CK/resrcs/syllabi/PDF/BritishandWorldLit.pdf>.

Core Knowledge Foundation. *Chemistry Syllabus*. PDF. (2002). 9 December 2002. <http://coreknowledge.org/CK/resrcs/syllabi/PDF/ChemistrySyllabus.pdf>.

Core Knowledge Foundation. *Children's Literature Syllabus*. PDF. (2002). 9 December 2002. <http://coreknowledge.org/CK/resrcs/syllabi/PDF/ChildrensLitSyllabus.pdf>.

Core Knowledge Foundation. *Composition and Grammar Syllabus*. PDF. (2002). 9 December 2002. <http://coreknowledge.org/CK/resrcs/syllabi/PDF/CompandGrammarSyllabus.pdf>.

Core Knowledge Foundation. *Composition and Grammar Syllabus: Appendices*. PDF. (2002). 9 December 2002. <http://coreknowledge.org/CK/resrcs/syllabi/PDF/CompandGrammarAppendices.pdf>.

Core Knowledge Foundation. *Earth Science Syllabus*. PDF. (2002). 9 December 2002. <http://coreknowledge.org/CK/resrcs/syllabi/PDF/EarthScienceSyllabus.pdf>.

Core Knowledge Foundation. *Geography Syllabus*. PDF. (2002). 9 December 2002. <http://coreknowledge.org/CK/resrcs/syllabi/PDF/GeographySyllabus.pdf>.

Core Knowledge Foundation. *Music Syllabus*. PDF. (2002). 9 December 2002. <http://coreknowledge.org/CK/resrcs/syllabi/PDF/MusicSyllabus.pdf>.

Core Knowledge Foundation. *Physics Syllabus*. PDF. (2002). 9 December 2002. <http://coreknowledge.org/CK/resrcs/syllabi/PDF/PhysicsSyllabus.pdf>.

Core Knowledge Foundation. *Teaching Beginning Reading Syllabus*. PDF. (2002). 9 December 2002. <http://coreknowledge.org/CK/resrcs/syllabi/PDF/TeachingReadingSyllabus.pdf>.

Core Knowledge Foundation. *U.S. History I (to 1865) Syllabus*. PDF. (2002). 9 December 2002. <http://coreknowledge.org/CK/resrcs/syllabi/PDF/USHistoryISyllabus.pdf>.

Core Knowledge Foundation. *U.S. History II (1865-1992) Syllabus*. PDF. (2002). 9 December 2002. <http://coreknowledge.org/CK/resrcs/syllabi/PDF/USHistoryIISyllabus.pdf>.

Core Knowledge Foundation. *World History I (to 1750) Syllabus*. PDF. (2002). 9 December 2002. <http://coreknowledge.org/CK/resrcs/syllabi/PDF/WorldHistoryISyllabus.pdf>.

Core Knowledge Foundation. *World History II (1750 to Present) Syllabus*. PDF. (2002). 9 December 2002. <http://coreknowledge.org/CK/resrcs/syllabi/PDF/WorldHistoryIISyllabus.pdf>.

Pawlikowska-Smith, Grazyna. *Canadian Language Benchmarks 2000:* Additional Sample Task Ideas. 2002. pdf. (April 2002): Centre for Canadian Language Benchmarks. <http://www.language.ca/pdfs/sampletasks.pdf>.

Pawlikowska-Smith, Grazyna. *Canadian Language Benchmarks 2000: Theoretical Framework*.

2002. pdf. (March 2002): Centre for Canadian Language Benchmarks. <http://www. language.ca/pdfs/final_theoreticalframework3.pdf>.

Cortazzi, Martin, and Wei Wei Shen. *Cross-Linguistic Awareness of Cultural Keywords: A Study of Chinese and English Speakers. Language Awareness*.2&3 (2001): 125-42 pp. 23 July 2007 <http://www.multilingual-matters.net/la/010/0125/la0100125.pdf>.

Council of Europe. *Common European Framework of Reference for Languages:* Learning, Teaching, Assessment--Case Studies.2002.

Council of Europe, and Council for Cultural Co-operation. Modern Languages Division. *Common European Framework of Reference for Languages:* Learning, Teaching, Assessment. Cambridge: Cambridge University Press, 2001.

Cuban, Larry. *Persistent Instruction: The High School Classroom, 1900-1980*. Phi Delta Kappan 64.2 (1982): 113-18.

Cummins, Jim. *Language, Power, and Pedagogy: Bilingual Children in the Crossfire*. Bilingual Education and Bilingualism; 23. Buffalo, NY: Multilingual Matters, 2000.

Cummins, Jim. *Negotiating Identities: Education for Empowerment in a Diverse Society*. 2nd ed. Los Angeles, CA: California Association for Bilingual Education, 2001.

Flinders, David J., and Stephen J. Thornton, eds. *The Curriculum Studies Reader*. 2nd ed. New York, NY: RoutledgeFalmer, 2004.

Freire, Paulo. *Pedagogy of the Oppressed*. Trans. Myra Bergman Ramos. New York, NY: Seabury Press, 1970.

Gagné, Robert Mills. *The Conditions of Learning*. New York, NY: Holt Rinehart and Winston, 1965.

Gardner, Howard. *Frames of Mind: The Theory of Multiple Intelligences*. New York, NY: Basic Books, 1983.

Gardner, Robert C., and Wallace E. Lambert. *Attitudes and Motivation in Second-Language Learning*. Rowley, MA: Newbury House Publishers, 1972.

Gatto, John Taylor. *Dumbing Us Down: The Hidden Curriculum of Compulsory Schooling*. New ed. Gabriola Island, BC: New Society Publishers, 2002.

Giles, Howard, and Robert N. St. Clair, eds. *Language and Social Psychology*. Oxford: B. Blackwell, 1979.

Hirsch, E. D., Jr. *The Knowledge Deficit: Closing the Shocking Education Gap for American Children*. Boston, MA: Houghton Mifflin, 2006.

Hunter, James Davison. *The Death of Character: Moral Education in an Age without Good or Evil*. 1st ed. New York, NY: Basic Books, 2000.

Kindell, Gloria Elaine, and M. Paul Lewis. *Assessing Ethnolinguistic Vitality: Theory and Practice: Selected Papers from the Third International Language Assessment Conference.*

Dallas: SIL International, 2000.

Krashen, Stephen D. *Principles and Practice in Second Language Acquisition.* Language Teaching Methodology Series. Toronto, ON: Pergamon Press, 1982.

Nisbett, Richard E. *The Geography of Thought: How Asians and Westerners Think Differently—and Why.* New York, NY: Free Press, 2003.

Munby, John. *Communicative Syllabus Design: A Sociolinguistic Model for Defining the Content of Purpose-Specific Language Programmes.* Cambridge, [Eng.]; New York: Cambridge University Press, 1978.

Pawlikowska-Smith, Grazyna, Canada. Citizenship and Immigration Canada, and Centre for Canadian Language Benchmarks. *Canadian Language Benchmarks 2000: English as a Second Language—for Adults.* Ottawa, ON: Citizenship and Immigration Canada, 2000.

Peterson, Christopher, and Martin E. P. Seligman. *Character Strengths and Virtues:* A Handbook and Classification. New York, NY: Oxford University Press, 2004.

Pinar, William F., ed. *International Handbook of Curriculum Research.* Mahwah, NJ: L. Erlbaum Associates, 2003.

Robertson, Heather-Jane. *No More Teachers, No More Books: The Commercialization of Canada's Schools. Toronto,* ON: M&S, 1998.

Ellis, Rod. *Second Language Acquisition.* Oxford Introductions to Language Study. Ed. H. G. Widdowson. Oxford England: Oxford University Press, 1997.

Ryan, Kevin, and James Michael Cooper. *Those Who Can Teach.* 10th ed. Boston, MA: Houghton Mifflin Co., 2004.

Sapon-Shevin, Mara. Playing Favorites: *Gifted Education and the Disruption of Community.* Albany, NY: State University of New York Press, 1994.

Tyler, Ralph Winfred, and University of Chicago. *Basic Principles of Curriculum and Instruction.* Chicago, IL: University of Chicago Press, 1949.

University of Calgary. Language Research Centre. *A Review of the Literature on Second Language Learning.* 2nd ed. Edmonton, AB: Alberta Education, 2006.

Vygotskiæi, L. S. *Thought and Language.* Cambridge, MA: M.I.T. Press, Massachusetts Institute of Technology, 1962.

Vygotskiæi, Lev Semeovich, and Michael Cole. *Mind in Society: The Development of Higher Psychological Processes.* Cambridge, MA: Harvard University Press, 1978.

Whitmore, Kathryn F., and Caryl G. Crowell. *Inventing a Classroom: Life in a Bilingual, Whole Language Learning Community.* York, ME: Stenhouse Publishers, 1994.